Two Stays in France

A Memoir

Walter James III

Copyright @ 2008 by Walter James III

All rights reserved. No part of this book may be reproduced or transmitted in any form or by any means, electronic or mechanical, including photocopying, recording, or by any information storage and retrieval system, without permission in writing from the author.

Cover design by author with outline of France and colors of the French flag inset with photos of the author while in France, the Eiffel Tower, ski trip with students, the school where the author taught, and some of the chief products of France – bread, cheese, grapes, and mineral water.

Special thanks to Bob Mutter for graphics on front cover

DEDICATION

This book is dedicated to all the teachers, students, and friends I met in France with a special tribute to those who still keep in touch with me after 20 years of first blessing me with their friendship (even though, in most cases, we haven't seen each other since I returned to the United States). This kind of friendship is to be cherished with much relish, for I must admit that it is indeed hard to find in America.

It is also dedicated to the teachers who are most responsible for teaching me the French language and culture – Mrs. Judy Cottone, my high school French teacher at South Florence High School in Florence, South Carolina; Dr. Joseph A. James, my French professor at Francis Marion College in Florence, South Carolina, who was the sole professor for all of my French classes and nominated me for the Modern Language Department Award which I received in my senior year; and the late Dr. George B. Daniel Jr. , the generous and comical professor of French at UNC-Chapel Hill, North Carolina, who obtained the scholarship for my first visit to France, directed the thesis for my master's degree in French literature, and recommended me for the teaching position in the French-American exchange program which enabled my second stay in France.

Preface

When one lives in a foreign country for several weeks or a few months, one begins to feel the pulse of that country. If one knows the language of that country, one can feel the pulse even stronger.

But, when one lives in a foreign country for six months or more, one begins to feel not only the pulse but the heartbeat of the country if one has a command of the language and lives among and interacts with its people. To hear and feel the heartbeat, one must talk to the people in their native tongue; eat with them; visit their homes; celebrate holidays with them; and participate in daily affairs such as going to the grocery store, the restaurants, the post office, the bank, the schools, the libraries, museums, places of worship, exhibitions, and other places that open the windows and shed light onto the country's culture.

It was to hear and feel the heartbeat of France and its culture as well as educational requirements that caused me to return to the country the second time and spend nine months there.

My initial visit the previous year was only five weeks. Since I had a good command of the language and lived with a family during my first visit, I had felt the pulse of the country very strongly. This could be attributed to my having studied the language, culture, and history of the country for nine years before this initial visit – four years in high school, four years in college, and one year at the master's degree level. Thus, I experienced little to no culture shock upon arrival.

Hopefully you can sense the pulse and heartbeat of France through my writing. My purpose in writing this book is threefold. First, I wish to preserve the memories and experiences of my two sojourns in the country while sharing them with my family and friends whether they be American, French, or of another nationality. Second, I wish to offer it as a tribute to the friends that I made and still have in France. Third, I wish to complete my autobiography, *From the Carolinas to Immortality*, which I published in 1997. In the chapter on my education in that book, I mentioned my trips to France and told the reader to see my publication on my stays there which I intended to publish shortly thereafter. Well, it's now 2008 and this publication is long overdue. Would you please forgive me for taking so long to return to my unfinished task?

With that said and off my mind and chest, I hope you find this memoir enjoyable, informative, relaxing, and inspiring as you travel with me while sitting quietly with it in your hands or share it with others while nibbling at a little *somethin' somethin'* or sipping from a little *somethin' somethin'*.

Come along with me to France and meet the people I encountered and the friends I made!

Table of Contents

PART ONE	**MY FIRST STAY**	
Chapter One	I'm Going to France!	11
Chapter Two	The Trip!	13
Chapter Three	Arriving in Paris	15
Chapter Four	Vichy	17
Chapter Five	Excursions	29
Chapter Six	Visiting Paris	33
Chapter Seven	Returning to the United States and My Studies	37
PART TWO	**MY SECOND STAY**	
Chapter Eight	I'm Going Back to Stay for A While!	43
Chapter Nine	Preparing for the Trip Back to France	49
Chapter Ten	Arrival in France and Return to Vichy	53
Chapter Eleven	Teaching at the College des Celestins	59
Chapter Twelve	French Friendships	81
Chapter Thirteen	Other Excursions in France	85
Chapter Fourteen	Other Experiences and Observations	89
Chapter Fifteen	The Change in Me	95
Appendix	*Journal Entries*	99

PART ONE: MY FIRST STAY

Chapter One – I'm Going to France!

I began studying French in the ninth grade at McClenaghan Junior High School in Florence, South Carolina, under Mrs. Hackney. I continued studying it for three years at South Florence High School under Mrs. Judy Cottone where I realized I had a knack for it after enjoying it so much. I decided to declare it as one of my majors at Francis Marion College in Florence, South Carolina, where Dr. Joseph A. James (not a relative) was my sole French professor; he asked me to serve as an assistant French instructor in one of his classes the summer after I graduated with my bachelor's degree. In my senior year in college, I decided to attend the University of North Carolina at Chapel Hill to continue studying the language and literature in graduate school after counseling with Dr. James about my plans for the future.

And now, finally, nearing the end of my first year of graduate school at UNC in 1987, I was told by one of my professors, Dr. George B. Daniel Jr., that he had obtained a scholarship for me to go and visit this country and be immersed in the language that I had studied for so long. Yes! I was going to France for five weeks! I would be going with a group of undergraduate students and some professors from North Carolina State University in Raleigh where the program was based. Not only would I get to visit the country, but I would also stay with a family, go to school, and visit Paris for four days.

Being a rather quiet and solitary individual, I was elated but cautiously optimistic about staying with a family. What if I didn't feel comfortable with them? Well . . . it would only last four weeks. And, it would be the best way for me to improve my speaking and auditory skills since I would have to communicate with them daily and be gently forced from spending all my social time with the Americans who had come with me in the program. I'd get a good view of French family life as we would talk and eat meals together. Of course, they might also like to know firsthand about life in America from my perspective.

With that in mind, I began to fill out the paperwork for my passport and visa and arrange matters for my first experience abroad. Since the stay would occur in the summer, there would be little inconvenience. I was living in a private dorm in Chapel Hill (Granville Towers) and would leave my car parked there. The few small bills I had would be paid in advance, and I'd be off to another world for a short while.

FRANCIS MARION COLLEGE

IN RECOGNITION OF OUTSTANDING ACADEMIC ACHIEVEMENT
IN THE DEPARTMENT OF MODERN LANGUAGES

WALTER JAMES, III

IS HEREBY NAMED RECIPIENT OF THE
MODERN LANGUAGE AWARD
BY THE FACULTY OF FRANCIS MARION COLLEGE
FOR THE 1984-1985 ACADEMIC YEAR

Department Chairman   *Dean of the College*

Above is my certificate of achievement as the top student in the Modern Languages department at Francis Marion College for the 1984-85 academic year.

Chapter Two – The Trip!

The day (June 26, 1987) came and I took a shuttle to the Raleigh-Durham airport (about 15 miles from Chapel Hill) to meet the group from North Carolina State University to catch my flight; this would be my first time flying. Since I arrived about an hour ahead of my flight time, I was one of the first persons at the airport in the group consisting of two French professors (one of whom was a French native) and about ten undergraduates whose comprehension of French ranged from one to four years of study.

The first leg of our flight was from Raleigh to New York on a Pan Am airline with a layover of several hours in New York before boarding an Air France jet that night for the trip across the Atlantic to Paris. The flight from Raleigh to the John F. Kennedy airport in New York took about one hour and twenty minutes (enough time to be served a snack of nuts and a drink). The surge of power felt as the plane sped for takeoff and lifted itself into the heavenly atmosphere above the mundane traffic and grounded streets and buildings thrilled my body and spirit.

Landing and disembarking at the John F. Kennedy airport in New York, however, brought me back to earth in a different world than I had left in Raleigh. There were so many people and different nationalities at the airport that it seemed as if every language under heaven was being spoken. People were dragging their luggage, looking for the gate for their next flight, trying to exit, trying to enter, standing in ticket lines, catching taxis, eating, talking, and just hustling and bustling in a flurry of rushed activity. Everything seemed so frantic and hurried that I wondered how the airport workers kept pace with it all to keep the flights moving in and out; a plane was landing and/or taking off every minute and flights were lined up on the runway for 30 to 45 minutes waiting their turn for takeoff. Lordy was I ever glad that I was with a group; otherwise, I would have been lost and not known where to go or what to do to catch my flight. Grabbing my luggage from the baggage area, I struggled to keep up with the group (my luggage had no wheels) as we wound our way through the maze of people to our gate for Air France. What a workout!!

That night as our jet took off for Paris I felt an even greater surge of power as the big jet (I think it was a 767) roared forward and upward towards its francophone destination. Soon we were served a meal and given pillows to accommodate our sleep on the six or seven hour journey. Falling asleep was not really a problem, but sleeping comfortably was a bit challenging even though there were three horizontal rows of seats on the plane which was only about half full. About two-thirds of the way across the ocean, the sunlight began peeking through the windows and most of us lowered the window shades to darken our sleep quarters or peeked briefly below at the distant blue before continuing our doze. It was dead nighttime in America, but as we approached France we entered a time zone that was six hours ahead of Eastern Standard Time in the United States. About two hours before landing, the flight attendants began handing out breakfast menus and moist hot napkins so we could wipe the sleep from our faces before we ate breakfast.

Chapter Three - Arriving in Paris

As our jet lowered, slowed, adjusted, and turned itself by degrees to land at the Charles de Gaulle airport in Paris, my eyes eagerly absorbed the French roofscape beneath the gray overcast skyscape. It was my first real view of France, and the first thing I noticed was that all the roofs seemed to have the same reddish clay color atop the light tan or grayish houses and buildings in their compact ground space. Making the final descent onto the runway, I again felt thrilled and awed as the powerful giant bird slowed, touched the runway, and broke its speed before coursing to the gate for disembarkation.

Once again, I was thankful to be with a group of people and with persons who had traveled to and within France several times; this smoothed the process of claiming baggage, going through customs, exchanging money, and catching a taxi from the airport to the train station. Even though I could speak French fluently, having this experience alone would have been quite stressful. It was now about 1 p.m. Our ride to the train station took about 20 minutes and a little less than 100 francs (about $15) per taxi. Since our train did not depart until 3 p.m., we ate at a restaurant in the station and watched the people coming and going. Our instructors then purchased tickets and we boarded the train and waited for it to depart for our final destination – Vichy. Ironically, this was also my first time riding a train; I found it to be not only a good cultural experience to see and interpret the actions and interactions of the people around me as I listened to their conversations to test my French comprehensive skills and ordered juice and snacks from the train's food cart but also a great way to see the

French countryside during the three and one-half hour ride from Paris (northern France) to Vichy (central France).

Riding the train through the countryside enlivened and quickened my mind to my studies of France's history; this was indeed an "old" country. I not only saw but felt like I was taken back in time with the old gray and black stone buildings and ruins from past centuries; suddenly I realized how new America was.

Finally, after three and one-half hours of traveling, stopping, eating, and sleeping the conductor announced that the next stop was Vichy.

Chapter Four – Vichy

Descending from the train with our luggage, we all took a few minutes to catch our breath and meet the different families with whom we would be staying. My host family was a middle aged lady, Madame Charlot, and her two sons (one of whom was with her). Before heading to their house, they gave me a short tour of the city. Riding through the streets, I sensed that Vichy was a medium-sized town that lacked the hustle-and-bustle atmosphere of Paris. I was thus pleased, because I wanted to be able to feel and absorb French life by interacting with people as much as possible. In most big cities, one is hurried and pushed through daily life with a sense of pressure and urgency that robs one of the pleasures of meeting and appreciating people, events, and nature. For me, this results in a void of impersonality at the end of the day.

We soon arrived at their home. It was a fairly large two-story apartment with a gated entrance and small flower garden in front. As Madame Charlot turned the key in the front door, I heard dogs barking loudly and someone telling them with little success to be quiet. Entering with my luggage, I was soon greeted by two rather large dogs which began barking loudly again. Somewhat fearful, I dropped my luggage to the floor and just stood there hoping that the dogs would not harm me. In her attempt to quiet them, Madame Charlot tried to assure me that I had no reason to fear as this was their way of greeting me.

I was soon shown to my room on the second floor which had a bed, a chest, and slanted ceiling. I got the impression that it had been part of the attic as the slanting prevented me from standing erect in one part of the room. After meeting

Madame Charlot's other son (they were approximately 9 and 11 years old) and her mother who lived downstairs, we had dinner. Afterwards, I walked downtown to meet with our group at a restaurant table on the sidewalk to relax and enjoy the nice, balmy, sunny Sunday evening and watch people as they walked and window-shopped. I then returned to the apartment to sleep as my body began to feel the six hour jetlag.

On Monday I arose and ate my first official French breakfast with Madame Charlot and her two sons. I found (as I was warned) that French breakfasts were very light, consisting only of toast or bread with jam or jelly or bread with butter or cheese and coffee, hot chocolate or juice. I'd have to supplement it with something from a patisserie or other shop on my way to school; I was sure I'd be hungry within an hour if this was all I ate for breakfast.

The apartment was close enough to the center of downtown so I could walk wherever I needed to go. I went to complete registration at the school I'd be attending

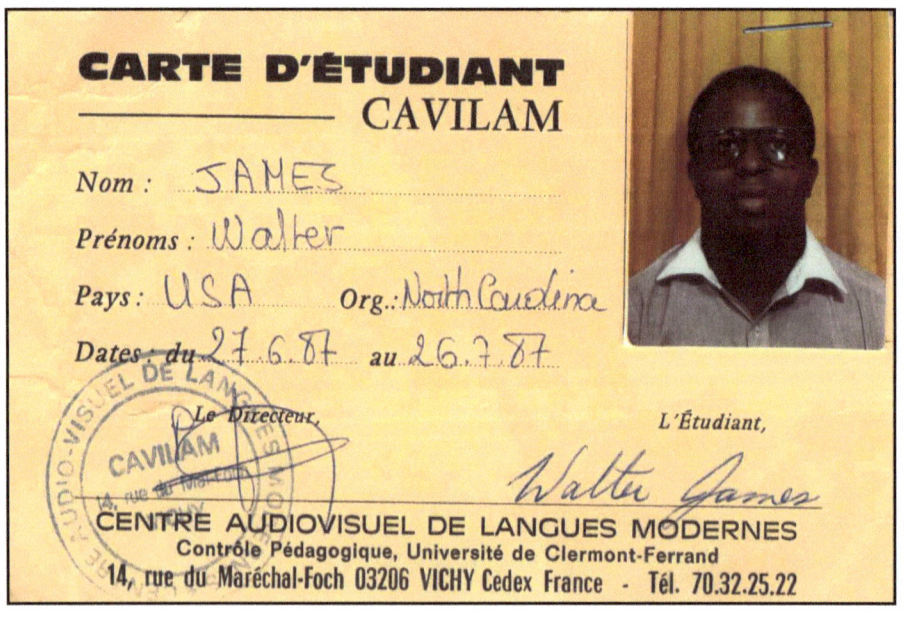

My student identification card at CAVILAM

(CAVILAM – Audio Visual Center for Modern Languages); after taking a placement test the following morning, I signed up for an advanced grammar and advanced conversation course.

I quickly became familiar with the town and found where my classes would be held and the location of the post offices, banks, public library, grocery store, shops, patisseries, etc. The town had a nicely landscaped park close to my apartment that was very long and bordered on a river (the Allier). The park was frequented by persons playing games, playing in the water sprinklers, relaxing, or just walking or running for exercise. Walking downtown and in the park, I soon realized that Vichy was kind of a ritzy place and had lots of retired persons who walked their dogs quite often. Not only did they walk them, but also took them inside the grocery stores, restaurants, banks or wherever they went. And even though the signs on the doors of the grocery stores or restaurants indicated that dogs were not allowed, there was such a large population of retirees who spent their money at these places that the rule was not enforced for fear that the owners would lose quite a bit of business. The ratio of dogs to people seemed to be one to three, and I had to constantly watch my step on the sidewalks to avoid stepping in the little 'gifts' that dogs were leaving as friendly reminders of their presence.

Also located in the park and other places around town were five or six stone enclosures that had fountains of mineral water which was free to the public; they were called sources (indicating sources of mineral water). People brought containers to these sources to fill and take back to their homes or drank directly from them. In fact, doctors sometimes recommended people from other places to stay in Vichy and consume the mineral water for a few weeks or a few months along with other therapy to recuperate from certain illnesses.

In addition to the many retirees and persons coming to Vichy for its mineral water, the most driving economical force was the school, CAVILAM, which not only brought money to the town but also gave the town an international flavor. I was shocked to learn that people from 164 different countries were currently at the school to either learn or improve their French so they could attend a francophone university or pursue some other venue that required knowledge of the French language. The diversity was very evident in my grammar class that began that Wednesday. There were less than 20 students but no less than six nationalities represented which included nine Italians (who were very talkative and gesticulative), three German, an Angolan, a Finn, a Japanese, myself (the only American), and a few other nationalities. Our instructor was a native Frenchwoman in her early thirties. Class began at 8:30 a.m. and ended at noon. Since French was the common language of everyone (for the most part), it forced us to speak totally in French during class and breaks. My conversation class consisted of about 15 persons and usually lasted approximately two hours in the afternoon; it was also very diverse and had several students from Japan.

Breakfast, class, lunch plus or minus a siesta, class, dinner, study or downtime, and sleep soon became my routine. However, I was surprised at the length of the days, even though it was summertime. In the United States, summer days begin with the sun peeking over the horizon at 5:30 a.m. and closing its curtains around 9 p.m. Here the sun began to send its rays forth at 5 a.m. and did not begin to withdraw its light until 10 p.m. If I was not exhausted from the day's activities, it was hard to go to sleep before 10:30 p.m. Lunchtime was usually from 12:00 to 1:30 or 2:00 depending on the day of the week. This gave everyone time for a siesta. Most shops and businesses except for restaurants closed for one and one-half to two hours to allow the owners and employees time to return home for lunch and take a nap if they so wished.

I also looked for and asked if there were any Protestant churches in town, since all the churches I saw were Catholic. From my studies, I knew that Catholicism was the predominant religion in France but thought there would be a smattering of other churches in the city. I finally found an Assembly of God church in the city. It was not exactly the type of church I had been attending in the United States, but I wanted to see the order of the service, the customs, see what version of the French Bible they were using, get a copy of the songbook, and see how much of the singing and preaching I could understand.

Normal attendance on a Sunday morning was between sixty and seventy-five persons. The service commenced with the congregation singing songs from the songbook and was led by the pastor who played his guitar along with one or two others; they also used drums and sometimes one or two tambourines. Occasionally, he would ask someone to stand and testify or give a word of encouragement. When he led them in prayer, the women would pull out scarves to cover their heads if they were not already wearing one or weren't wearing a hat. The pastor, ministers, and some of the other men wore neckties, but many of the people were casually dressed. Though almost everyone was modestly dressed, some of the ladies wore pants. An offering was received about midway through the service. I found that I understood all of the singing when I followed along in the songbook but understood only about seventy-five percent if the song was not in the songbook; words are pronounced and accentuated differently in singing than when they are spoken. I could understand ninety percent of the preaching and learned a lot of new vocabulary since the Biblical language and expressions used in sermons included lots of words that were not used in everyday life (as is the case in the English language). They used the Louis Segond version of the Bible whereas the French Bible most obtainable in America (which I had brought with me) was the ecumenical version.

The pastor and church members were neither unkind nor too friendly. The pastor and some of the members would shake hands after church and after finding that I and some of the other students from CAVILAM could speak French would ask what country and city we were from, how we liked Vichy, and would express their welcome. One or two members asked if we'd like to get a bite to eat and chat sometimes.

One Sunday upon my return from church, Madame Charlot's mother asked me if I had been to church when she saw what appeared to be books in my hand. When I responded positively, she asked me what type of church it was and upon finding that it was a Protestant church told me that there was a small Baptist church as well as a Jehovah Witness gathering nearby. She then began telling me about the Catholic church, its saints, the priests, etc. and tried to convince me that it was the true church. She believed that one had to go through the priests to communicate with God. I talked with her about ten to fifteen minutes to see how much knowledge she had of the Bible. She mostly referred to Old Testament Scriptures and her Catholic book when she talked. I asked her if she understood the significance of the renting of the veil in the temple when Jesus died. That is, it signified that everyone could approach God directly and no longer needed a priest to intercede for them as in the Old Testament. She didn't comment much on this. She indicated that she was a strong Catholic but acknowledged that I knew the Bible quite well. I enjoyed conversing with her but didn't get a chance to talk with her much more before I left Vichy.

It was great to be totally immersed in the French culture and language; everyday routines were learning experiences because I would see or hear new words or expressions, taste new foods, or meet new people in Vichy or from another country. My classes were not difficult, but I had to sometimes read through the instructions for exercises slowly and then look at the directions given by my instructor twice before doing the exercises since the instructions and directions were not always clear. I sometimes returned to the apartment for lunch but often ate at an inexpensive restaurant with persons from my American group or some of my classmates. I really enjoyed the long lunch periods that allowed me to catch a nap before my afternoon class; I soon realized how much energy my body and mind were using by being immersed in a foreign culture. Even though I knew the language, my brain used more energy in comprehension and translating responses than I realized which resulted in my feeling slightly wearier than normal at the end of the day. I also got plenty of exercise from walking to and from class and walking to take care of errands or just strolling in the park for relaxation. Breakfast and dinner were provided by Madame Charlot since my tuition included two meals provided by my host family. Dinner was always served in courses. First, there was a salad which usually consisted of lettuce and salad oil, then meat and vegetables, cheese, and last a fruit or dessert.

At meals, I became accustomed to a few things which were not "un-American" but which my family had never done in the United States. First, we never allowed pets inside our house, and secondly I had never eaten inside a restaurant or a house where dogs were allowed to sit on the floor at the table while a meal was being served. I soon learned that the two dogs in the apartment were mother and daughter. The mother was brown with small black markings and the daughter, who was quite energetic and expecting puppies, was black. They usually sat on the floor by the table while we ate and were often handed bits of food by the two boys. When cheese was served, the mother dog would quietly groan until she was given a small serving. The presence of dogs at the table during mealtime curved my appetite, and I ate only enough to kill my hunger.

Upon my return from school one day, I learned that the younger dog had given birth to eight puppies in a closet room downstairs. This was her first litter and since she was constantly nursing, she was often hungry. One day Madame Charlot invited a former student and his wife to dinner and decided to use the larger dining room downstairs. She exerted much effort in preparing the meal and placed some sliced meat on a serving tray on a cart in the dining room to expedite time. Unfortunately, she forgot to close the door completely while she finished the meal in the kitchen. When we all sat down to eat and started to pass the plate of meat around, she realized that the young dog had been in the room earlier and eaten two or three slices of meat from the tray. She was visibly upset but decided to serve the meat from the tray anyway. I was shocked, because I thought that the remaining meat would either be thrown away or at least placed on a different tray. Almost everyone accepted a serving, but when it came to me I said *Non, merci* (No thanks).

One evening she made an apricot pie for dinner which was quite tasty. Since we did not eat it all, it was left on the table for the following day. When one of the boys lifted a slice the next evening, ants came from underneath; he just brushed them off and ate. This took my appetite and I went to my room.

I talked mostly with Madame Charlot and her sons when we were eating. She usually prepared meals, but occasionally we would go to restaurants. I learned that she was a widow and hosted students to supplement her income and give her kids exposure to persons of other cultures. She did her best to ensure that I had opportunities to experience as much as possible of the French culture. On Bastille Day (July 14 – similar to America's Independence Day), I went with the family to see the fireworks. She also took me to historical exhibitions and celebrations - one of which was at a nearby castle that was constructed in the thirteenth century.

One evening we went to dinner at a couple's house who were friends of hers in Vichy. This was my first introduction to an invitational dinner, and it was quite an experience. When one is invited to dinner at someone's home, it is usually on Thursday, Friday, or Saturday. One is expected to arrive about 8 p.m. and bring a small gift, be it a flower or some other item that one thinks the host would appreciate. The prelude to the dinner begins by talking in the lounge or family room where appetizers are served. About 9 p.m., one is requested to come to the dining table where the meal is served in courses with much talking between each course. By 10 or 10:30 p.m., one has usually finished the meal. At this point, one remains at the table and engages in very lively discussions on topics ranging from politics, international affairs, philosophy, education, religion, or whatever subject comes up. These discussions usually end between 11:30 p.m. and 12:00 a.m. and one departs for home. Such dinners can only be held on Thursdays, Fridays, or Saturdays because Friday is the last workday of the week, and the hosts and guests usually do not work on the weekend.

The discussion after dinner at this couple's home was one of the liveliest discussions I had ever witnessed in a home because of the different backgrounds of the couple. The husband was Arab and of the Muslim faith while the wife was French and Catholic. They had four children who were all grown, professionals, and on their own except for the youngest who was eighteen and had just completed high school; he was an atheist. In addition, they had a little Dachshund in the house who barked quite furiously when the discussions became heated. Their discussion on religion and politics was so intense that I thought they were indeed angry with each other. My face portrayed my dismay, and the mother asked me if I was all right. When I told them I had never been in the midst of such an intense discussion, she said, "We're not upset with each other but just voicing our opinions. This is nothing; you should be here when all four of the children are here. The discussions are so intense that I go under the table; the dog just goes outside." I couldn't imagine it being more intense and was further stunned to learn that they weren't even trying to prove anything or even reach a conclusion; they were debating for the sake of debating. They were going in circles and were enjoying it.

Later as I reflected on this style of circular debating after visiting France again the following year, I realized how much language, thought processes, and street designs are interrelated as I mentally compared French and American cultures. English grammar is very linear in that a sentence usually follows the chronological pattern of subject, verb, direct object, and indirect object with adjectives and adverbs which modify those parts of speech immediately preceding or following them. In America, when we debate our goal is to prove a point and convince our opponent or audience to believe us or take our side. Our street system reflects this linear goal-oriented mentality in that most of our streets run parallel or perpendicular to each other and eventually connect to major highways. French grammar, however, is less linear in that subjects, verbs, and indirect objects follow a fairly consistent chronological order and adjectives usually follow the part of speech they modify, but all nouns are masculine or feminine and several nouns change meaning depending on their gender. In addition, several adjectives can change meaning depending on their position (preceding or following) to the noun they modify and must agree in number and gender with the nouns they modify. Adverbs can also be more or less emphatic depending on their location within a sentence. In addition, there are almost as many exceptions as rules in French grammar. In sum, the French language is a more subjective language than the English language. Just as the lineation of the English language subconsciously invokes us to prove a point when debating with family, friends, or acquaintances, the subjectivity of the French language invokes the Frenchmen to circular debate in such circumstances. Similarly, many of their streets and intersections are circular and less perpendicular and parallel than the streets in America.

Observing such interactions within the homes and everyday lives of people caused me to feel the pulse of the people and the language. I also noticed the pride that they took in their language. Because there were so many tourists in Paris, most people in the shops and vendors on the sidewalk could speak English. However, as one moved away from Paris, it was essential to know French to communicate. People appreciated one's attempt to speak French even if one was not fluent or made grammatical errors. However, shopkeepers or the person one stopped on the street would politely correct one's grammar by saying the sentence, phrase, or word correctly. In America, however, if a grammatical mistake in conversation does not hinder comprehension, one seldom tries to correct a person's grammar in everyday conversation or in an informal situation.

Such cultural benefits were the rewards and perks of my living in a small city.

Chapter Five – Excursions

One of the advantages of attending the school, CAVILAM, was the option of taking weekend excursions to different parts of France at discounted prices on a nice comfortable bus provided by the school.

I took two of these day trips. On my first excursion, I went to the city of Lyon which is one of the larger cities in southeastern France and is known as the capital of French cuisine. We had a tour guide on the bus who told us much of the history of the city and pointed out significant places and statues. Afterwards, I ate and walked through the downtown area before returning to the bus which took us past the Rhone River (one of the five major rivers in France). Before departing from the city, we visited a beautiful park which had many ducks, swans, and geese as well as a mini zoo with caged and fenced animals such as bears, bison, monkeys, giraffes, elephants, goats, chickens, and some exotic birds.

On the second trip, I traveled through the countryside of Auvergne (the region in which Vichy and the department of Allier are located). France is divided into 95 departments as the United States is divided into 50 states. The countryside was gorgeous and very pastoral with lots of open spaces of rolling hills, pastures, and peacefully grazing cows. We stopped for lunch at a restaurant located in the mountainous countryside; I was very hungry and ready to eat. The inside of the restaurant was simple and clean with picnic-like tables covered with red checkered tablecloths. The owner of the restaurant (a middle-aged lady) and her staff were ready for our group which consisted of 30 to 50 persons from CAVILAM and kept them busy. Serving the meal in courses, she kept asking us "Vous aimez? Vous aimez?" (Do you like it? Do you like it?). I tasted goat meat for the first time in a salad she served and found it rather tasty though slightly pungent. I was so hungry that I had seconds; she also brought five different kinds of cheeses for us to eat. Cheese is one of the courses served with almost every French meal; each region of France is known for its type of cheese which varies depending on the land and the type of cows or goats from which the cheese is produced. We spent about an hour and a half at the restaurant before touring more of the countryside.

Note: On the following page is my certificate from CAVILAM which certifies that I completed the coursework and linguistic, cultural, and civilization requirements offered through the program in which I was enrolled while being immersed in the French language and culture.

Centre Audio-Visuel de Langues Modernes

CONTROLE PÉDAGOGIQUE: UNIVERSITÉS de CLERMONT

Département: Institut International de langue, civilisation et culture françaises

Nous attestons que Monsieur *James Walker* a suivi avec assiduité les Cours du Centre Audio-Visuel de Langues Modernes de Vichy, pendant la période du 29 juin 1987 au 24 juillet 1987.

La Responsable du Département,
Jacqueline NAVARRO

Le Chargé de Mission des Universités de Clermont
Max DANY
Agrégé de l'Université

VICHY

Chapter Six – Visiting Paris

At the end of my four weeks in Vichy, I had gained new confidence in my ability to talk with French native speakers and perform daily tasks and errands with ease. I liked Vichy but was ready for a change of scenery and some new challenges. Thus, it was with delighted anticipation that I boarded the train in Vichy with the others from the North Carolina State group for the final part of the stay - four days in Paris. The native French profesor who had come from North Carolina State University with us had traveled to another city to spend time with her family while we were in Vichy and was to meet us in Paris. We were yearning to finally tour Paris and then go home. Our flight into Paris and direct transport to the train station when we first arrived had given us little time to see anything; we had only felt the hustle and bustle of the big city.

Arriving in Paris, we checked into a youth hostel which was a discounted lodging facility for international students under 26 years of age. As we left the train station and ventured onto the streets of Paris this time, I began to realize how many Americans were in Paris. They were easily spotted by their actions (usually in groups) and their conversation (Someone would call or yell out "Hey yall, over here!"). I heard English four times before I heard French after departing from the train. I soon realized that one could get around in Paris fairly easily without knowing French. Since it was a tourist city, most of the people in the shops, restaurants, and places of business spoke enough English to do a transaction, give directions, and have a brief conversation with Anglophones.

That afternoon and the next two days, we had a guide who met us for tours and directed us to restaurants. She knew the metro, where to go to obtain discounts and the location of souvenir shops that were less expensive than those on the main thoroughfares frequented by tourists, and the location of several restaurants that we could afford as students. She was friendly but became slightly exasperated with a few of us because we asked so many questions about life in Paris and asked for more details about some of the monuments we visited since we had studied them in our French classes. At one restaurant where we had pizza, the waitress became rude since our group was so big (ten to twelve persons) and kept asking for more water since the glasses were so small. Finally, the waitress said (in French), "I might as well bring you the tap to drink from." Our guide became agitated and stuck her tongue out at the waitress when she left the table; for some reason the waitress spun back around and caught her sticking her tongue out while making a face at her. She quickly turned and went her way. When she brought the bill, most of the group decided to leave her ½ francs (similar to leaving pennies) to show her what they thought of her service.

We had a much better experience one night when our group went to a restaurant near the nineteenth century church Sacre-Coeur where we had crepes and apple cider for dinner. Hmmmm!!!! We all ate the warm crepes and drunk the delicious apple cider till we were stuffed. It was about 11 p.m. when we finished the meal and the group decided to walk back to the youth hostel. We were all glad to be in a group since Paris seemed to have a number of deranged people on the streets at night who thought nothing of approaching persons alone or in groups and asking for money or offering other services.

During the day, Paris is quite safe and has an air of romance (despite its hurried atmosphere) as artists and booksellers paint and sell their drawings, books, and flowers beside the Seine River, and the old gothic monuments such as Notre Dame display their historic grace and beauty in the background while the Eiffel Tower points its magnificent steel finger at the sky. At night, however, this atmosphere continues to hover but is mixed with precaution as one encounters more persons walking the streets (even on the main thoroughfares) who seem mentally disturbed or have unashamed faces about their intentions.

Even though we visited quite a few of the well-known sites in Paris with our guide during the day, I still had not seen all the monuments I wanted to see after three days. Thus, on the fourth day I mapped out a route which combined taking the metro and walking to see the sites I had not seen. I did not know how soon I'd be back in France and was determined to see as many of the places and monuments I'd studied about for so many years while here. I set out on my own and went to see the Eiffel Tower (though the line was too long for me to go up into it), the Champs Elysees and the Arc de Triomphe, went inside the Louvre, and stopped at several smaller monuments and famous sites along the way. Aching so badly I could hardly walk after about six hours, I returned to the youth hostel tired but satisfied.

Laying in my bed that night, I realized that I was not only physically tired but was also beginning to feel emotionally and mentally fatigued from being in the hustle and bustle of a city that never really slept. I could hear car brakes screeching to a halt, car horns honking, and car motors roaring into the wee hours of the morning. Hearing such noises constantly while lapsing in and out of sleep did not allow me to rest as fitfully as I desired, and I was ready for a quieter place after seeing so many of the things I had heard about and studied for years.

During our stay in Paris, we also took a half-day trip less than one-half hour from Paris to visit Versailles, the palace constructed by Louis X1V (one of France's most well-known kings often referred to as the Sun King who reigned from 1643 to 1715). With its hall of mirrors, elegant chambers, and beautiful paintings, it looked just as luxurious and exquisite as the pictures I had seen of it. The gardens and grounds were also beautiful with their linear patterns and designs and full of tourists. According to history, it was Louis XIV's elaborate spending that later led to the French Revolution in 1789 during the reign of Louis XVI who was king from 1774 to 1793.

This break from Paris was a nice breather. In two days it was time to board the flight back home.

Chapter Seven – Returning to the United States and My Studies

Waiting at the airport for our flight on Air France from Paris to New York, we had all enjoyed our stay for the most part but were also a little homesick and ready to see our family and friends and talk about our experience. The journey back over the Atlantic and into New York at the JFK airport did not produce as sleepy a feeling as our first journey since it was continuous daytime and we were traveling backwards in time. During airtime we were served lunch and dinner and moved around talking with each other. Landing in New York, we got our luggage and headed for the Pan Am flight back to Raleigh where we landed in the evening. I caught a shuttle back to Chapel Hill and phoned my parents to let them know that I had returned safely and would be coming home to South Carolina soon to tell them about my experience.

When I went home several days later, one of the first things my parents commented on was my weight loss. "How much weight did you lose? Looks like your back pockets are about to shake hands," my mother said. I told her that I hadn't weighed but had probably lost about ten pounds, since my appetite was curved by often having dogs sitting on the floor by the table while I ate. "You've lost more than that," she said. I realized that I had lost some weight since my pants were loser, but didn't fully realize how much the downward curve in my appetite, constant walking, and expending of mental energy had decreased my weight. When I went to my home church that Sunday, one of the older sisters commented on my weight loss and said, "Glad to see you! You come back looking *po*."

I soon returned to Chapel Hill since the fall semester would start in a few weeks. I would not only be taking classes for the second and final year of my master's degree program, but I would also be teaching at the university for the first time and had to attend teacher orientation in my department before classes began. During my first year, I had been awarded a research assistantship which only required me to work eight to ten hours per week helping three professors with their research projects. I was indeed glad that I had been awarded this assistantship in my first year of graduate school since it allowed me more time to concentrate on my classes (which were intense and required heavy reading) while I adjusted to graduate school and its requirements and expectations.

This second year would be different and more challenging as I would be balancing teaching, studying, and working a part-time job on the weekends since my teaching stipend would be less than the research stipend from the previous year. Like many of the other graduate students in my departments, I would have full responsibility for teaching a class while studying full-time and would constantly feel the battle of giving my best to the students as a teacher and being a good student myself to ensure that my grades did not suffer.

At the end of teacher orientation (which lasted a few days), I was assigned to teach French I (first semester of elementary French) since this was my first year of teaching. I was pleased but somewhat nervous as I thought of stepping into a college classroom for the first time with full responsibility for class instruction, grades, etc. However, my fresh and firsthand experience in France and the props I had brought back with me to use in class as hands-on material gave me the courage I needed to do the job. I had between twenty and twenty-seven students who were almost all freshmen and seemed eager to learn when they entered class at nine o'clock in the morning. They gave their best, caused no problems, and were drawn to learning French (even if they only took it as a requirement when enrolling) when I gave them real French menus, metro maps, train schedules, etc. to use when we did group activities such as ordering from a café menu, taking the metro to see different monuments in Paris, or deciding which train to take from Paris to another city. At the end of the semester, I was somewhat exhausted from balancing teaching and my studies but was very pleased with the comments that my students wrote on their class evaluations.

PART TWO: MY SECOND STAY

Chapter Eight – I'm Going Back to Stay for A While!

In the spring semester, I was assigned to teach French Two (second semester of elementary French) at eight o'clock in the morning. Since some students were not quite awake and were not yet speaking clearly in their native tongue at that hour, I tried to do as many group exercises and use hands-on materials whenever possible to keep the class alive and alert. This was more challenging than the previous semester since most of the students were now second-semester freshmen, had learned the ropes of college life, knew how quizzes and tests were graded in our department, and how much effort they had to expend to obtain the grade they wanted or needed. In addition, French II was more challenging than French I since it included more grammar even though there were still cultural lessons included. I was very glad I had lots of props and visual aids from France to use during class since this awakened many of them out of their semi-sleep when we did exercises.

As for my studies, I was under a lot of pressure. This was the final semester of my degree program, and even though I had completed my course requirements, I had to take my comprehensive written exams and do a thesis to complete my requirements for the master's degree. Classes had started in early January and my written exams were scheduled for mid-February. I had to prepare to be tested on the six major periods of French literature – the Middle Ages, sixteenth century, seventeenth century, eighteenth century, nineteenth century, and twentieth century. I had taken a class in each of the six periods and had also done as much reading as possible from the reading list given to me when I arrived the previous year. Approximately two weeks before the exams, the department would give me the option to choose two periods and I would have to draw to determine which of the other two periods I would be tested on. I decided to choose the sixteenth and seventeenth centuries since I felt most knowledgeable about them; the drawings resulted in me also being tested on the eighteenth and nineteenth centuries. I was relieved since the Middle Ages did not appeal to me as much as the other periods, and the twentieth century literature was rather depressing as it reflected the mood of France after the two world wars and was rather atheistic. The examinations lasted for two days, but the stress of studying for them left me so mentally exhausted that I could not do any serious academic work for a month afterwards other than prepare for and teach my class. I still had to write my thesis but did not fully collect my thoughts and prepare to write until the latter part of March.

Knowing that the process of writing, submitting each chapter for approval to my thesis advisor (Dr. George B. Daniel Jr.) as I wrote, and correcting and editing after his comments and suggestions would take longer than a month (when the deadline for submitting the thesis to the graduate school in order to graduate in May would be upon me), I resigned myself to the fact that I would have to finish during the summer.

However, I had to make plans for the upcoming year. Should I consider continuing to the doctoral level? Should I begin job searching? Or should I apply for one of the positions our department offered in France? One thing was sure; I needed some sort of mental break. I began to analyze my options. Our department had several positions available abroad which were offered every year and came with stipends – one was a teacher's position at the HEC (a business school in Paris) where one would teach business English and conversation to French students; one was a teacher exchange position in a French middle school or high school for teaching English and American culture and offered the applicant three preferences as to the city or town in which he/she preferred to teach (the applicant had to be between 20 and 30 years old but preferably no older than 26); another position was a three month stay in which one could work on a research project related to one's academic interest. The fourth option was to serve as the Program Assistant for the UNC Junior Year Abroad program for nine months. One would accompany the students from New York to Montpellier (site of program in France) and assist the Resident Director of the students and teach English, Civilization, Literature or Linguistics. Since I was twenty-four, needed a break from studying, would have to spend six months in France or some other francophone country to fulfill requirements for the doctorate if I decided to pursue it, I decided to apply for the middle/high school position. I also liked the idea of choosing the location in which I would teach, though it was not guaranteed but would be given strong consideration.

Since I would be going alone this time if I returned, I submitted Vichy as my first choice since I was already familiar with the city. Since it was in the center of France, I could travel to other parts of France at the most reasonable cost and use my educational discount card to reduce my expenses at many places throughout France. And of course (as I stated previously), it was a small to medium sized city (30,000 to 40,000 persons including the adjacent town of Cusset) with an international flavor because of the language school, CAVILAM. My second and third choices were

Toulouse, a larger city in southwestern France and Aix-en-Provence in southern France. In addition to my preference, my placement also depended on whether a position was available in the cities I had listed.

I interviewed for the position with some of the faculty members and a previous participant in the teacher exchange program in March (if I remember correctly). Since there were not many applicants for the positions, I felt rather confident that my request would be granted. The interviewers asked the reason for my desiring the position, how I would respond to certain questions about American life and culture, if there was anything that would prevent me from staying the entire eight months of the exchange program, or if I might feel homesick and want to return early. The interview was fairly informal but allowed the committee to ascertain whether I was a serious applicant, to assess my views on certain aspects of American life, and to hear how I would use my teaching skills to relate life in America to teenagers of another country. Within approximately two weeks, I found that I had been granted the position. Shortly afterwards, I was informed that I had also been assigned to a middle school in Vichy which was my first choice. I was inwardly excited but also nervous but had little time to be overtaken by either emotion, since my immediate task was to finish my thesis before departing in September.

In April I began writing my thesis on the seventeenth century religious French poet, Jean de la Ceppede. I decided to do an analysis of color symbolism in his poems. Once the semester ended, I worked at the Town of Chapel Hill full-time during the day in the personnel department and worked third shift at Granville Towers part-time as a desk attendant. I wrote much of my thesis on third shift after I had finished my nightly duties.

Chapter Nine – Preparing for the Trip Back to France

By the end of August as the campus was revving up for another semester, my thesis was basically finished and Dr. George B. Daniel and my thesis committee which included two readers (professors in sixteenth and seventeenth century literature) had approved it for submission for publication through the Graduate School (a normal part of the process) after recommendations for minor changes and editing. Tired but aching to finish everything before my departure for France in mid-September, I hurriedly made the changes. At one point I couldn't get WordPerfect to indent all the paragraphs correctly (because of some quirk) in the eighty-nine page document and requested the help of the personnel (Camelia Brooks and Joyce Smith) with whom I had worked at the Town of Chapel Hill during the summer since they used the program daily. Thanks to them (and Joyce going paragraph by paragraph to correct the format), I finally submitted the thesis to the graduate school.

My presentation and defense of the thesis were set for September 19 with my thesis committee which consisted of my advisor and the other two readers. This would be the first time I had ever faced a committee of professors for an oral examination. Not only did I have to present my thesis and explain my reason for using the reference sources and other questions they posed about it, but I also had to do a literary analysis of a short text which they had given me the day before and be tested orally on French culture and civilization. I was nervous but knew that they were satisfied with the thesis and would not have approved it with the suggested changes nor allowed me to defend it if there were major problems. I just hoped that I would pass the other parts since they could throw anything they wished at me.

The defense and examination lasted little more than an hour. They then left the room to huddle; soon they came back and congratulated me for passing and completing the degree and recommended me to continue for the doctoral degree. Elated and relieved, I thanked them and went to relax. My mind now turned to making final preparations for the trip back to France.

In the early summer, I had received a postcard from one of the administrators, Madame Feuillat, at the school in Vichy where I would be teaching. I later received another letter welcoming me and informing me that arrangements had been made for me to live at a private hotel next door to the school.

I had worked hard during the summer to pay off most of my bills so I wouldn't have to worry with making payments while overseas. I would be paid by the French government for teaching and would have enough to live on but wouldn't have a lot left to spend. I also had to pay for my plane ticket. The Raleigh-Durham Airport had begun a direct flight to Paris with American Airlines since my last trip, and I was advised to buy a standby ticket which was less expensive than a normal ticket. To do this, I had to begin calling the airline three days before I needed to depart to see if they had seats that were not booked. I had asked my parents if they would keep my car during my stay so I drove home to leave my car and other few belongings with them in South Carolina. This also gave me some time with them and my siblings before leaving the country. I needed to leave on Saturday, September 24, since my teacher orientation in France would be held mid-week.

I had little trouble getting a ticket since the flight was rarely full on the weekend. My parents drove me to the Raleigh Durham airport. After saying goodbye and feeling rather choked in the throat, I boarded the plane and was soon off to France again.

Chapter Ten – Arrival in France and Return to Vichy

Joyful about the nonstop flight which saved me from having to deal with the hustle and bustle of changing planes in New York and thankful for the experience of the previous flight to France, I ate the meal served and soon fell asleep as the plane made its way across the ocean. An hour or so before landing, we were served breakfast. The flight was six to seven hours long and quite smooth except for a few air pocket bumps.

We soon prepared to land at the Orly airport in Paris which was smaller than the Charles de Gaulle airport where I had landed on my previous trip. After retrieving my luggage, I went through customs, exchanged some money, and caught a taxi to the train station where I purchased a ticket to Vichy. Since I took the same train route as my first trip, there was not much scenery I hadn't seen before so I dozed but occasionally wakened to ensure my baggage was still with me.

My train ticket from Paris to Vichy

Stepping off the train in Vichy, I looked around and waited for a few minutes to see if I saw anyone who seemed to be expecting me. I had received a card stating that the owner of the hotel would meet me at the station. Seeing no one who seemed to be waiting or watching for anyone, I took a taxi to the hotel which was less than five minutes away.

Entering the lounge room of the hotel, I met the owner, Monsieur Caron, who welcomed me and said, "Well, if we knew you were a black boy we would have known who you were at the train station and you wouldn't have had to take a taxi. We were waiting for you." He said this in English and I found that his English was pretty good after talking with him briefly. So he and his wife had been waiting at the train station but didn't know who I was when I got off the train. I didn't sense any degradation in his voice and didn't respond to the comment. I had purposely not mentioned that I was black in my correspondence with the school or the hotel, since I was unsure of the racial climate at the school, how I would be received at the hotel, or the overall racial climate in France. I had been treated nicely during my previous stay with Madame Charlot and her sons but knew that persons who opened their homes to students were probably more welcoming of other nationalities than the general population. However, in the coming weeks and months, I soon learned that I had little to fear. I found that France loved black Americans; in fact I was respected and treated better than in the United States.

Monsieur Caron showed me to my room and gave me the key. It was a spacious room on the second floor with a bed, small dresser, closet, and small kitchen area with a mini refrigerator. He then gave me a quick tour of the hotel and informed me of the rules. He and his wife owned the three story hotel which had a total of nineteen rooms on the first and second floors. They lived on the third floor. The lounge on the first floor was available for relaxing and talking.

I phoned home and told my Dad that I had arrived safely. "Are you in Paris?" he asked. "No sir, I'm already at my final destination in Vichy, about three and one-half hours below Paris," I said. He seemed a little surprised that I had arrived so quickly. I chatted briefly with him and then went to unpack my luggage.

Relaxing in the lounge that evening I met Madame Caron and some of the other occupants and found that most of them attended CAVILAM and were there for several weeks or a few months and were from other countries such as Turkey, India, China, etc. A few were actually French and were attending nearby technical or specialty schools. I learned that one of the occupants, whose name was Hazel, was from England and was also there to teach English but would be teaching in a high school in an adjacent town. Every year the person who came from abroad to teach English at the school next door where I would be teaching roomed here. I began to sense that the hotel had a family atmosphere; I already enjoyed talking with the other occupants and the owners. Almost everyone was forced to speak French since that was the common language among us.

I soon headed to my room. The long trip and its preparations dropped me into a fitful sleep, but I kept dreaming that I was still on the airplane.

The next day I went next door to the school, the College des Celestins, where I would be teaching and met the principal and some of the administrators. They were all cordial and very welcoming and were excited to have someone from America, since the English teacher from abroad usually came from Great Britain. The school was an old high-rise white building that was seven to eight stories tall with the cafeteria and other rooms on the first floor. Administrative offices were on the second

View from my hotel. In center is the city's public library and to the far right is the school (College des Celestins) where I taught.

floor and the library was located on the third floor. Most of the classrooms were located on the second floor and above. In addition to the principal, assistant principal, and secretaries, I also met the librarian, Mademoiselle Arlette Janiaud, who was very cordial; the following week she brought me a box of materials to look through that previous English teachers from abroad had left. After this brief introduction, I returned to my hotel.

Hotel where I lived while teaching

Chapter Eleven – Teaching at the College des Celestins

The following day I boarded the train for my orientation at a university in Clermont-Ferrand, a larger city about forty-five minutes south of Vichy. Clermont-Ferrand was quite lively but yet very historic with its university students and a thirteenth century cathedral which was a tourist attraction. It was also majestically bordered with volcanic mountains (the Puy de Dome) which could be seen from almost anywhere in the city. I stayed at one of the modern university dormitories during the few days of orientation.

Teacher orientation in Clermont-Ferrand

At orientation, there were over 100 of us in the auditorium. We were all from different countries, of course, and were there to teach English or Spanish. Of all the persons present, I only met one other person who was from the United States – a girl from Georgia. To ensure that we all understood the French school system, one of the speakers briefly explained how the system worked and at what level students began learning foreign languages. We were also informed of paperwork we needed to complete and submit to the local government in the cities where we were teaching so there would be a record of our employment if we needed medical care and so we could claim the appropriate benefits from the French government once we reached retirement age. That drew a chuckle from some of us, because we wondered how much we would receive from teaching in the system for only a year. In addition, the speakers gave us some ideas and suggestions for use in the classroom.

When I returned to Vichy that week, I took care of the paperwork at the local government office and some other business such as opening a checking account at the local bank. Since my duties at the school did not officially begin until October (the following week), I had time to plan activities that I would use in the classroom. In addition, I had time to catch up on the sleep I had missed during the summer. For the first month, I slept for one or two hours during the day in addition to sleeping seven or eight hours at night; my body and mind were exhausted from working two jobs and writing my thesis during the summer months.

Before going into further detail about teaching, I'd like to briefly explain the structure of the French educational system. Children attend maternal school (nursery-kindergarten) from three to six years of age. From six to eleven years of age, they attend primary school which is the equivalent of the American elementary school. From eleven to fifteen, they attend "college" which is the equivalent of the American middle school formerly known as junior high school. They must pass an exit exam from middle school before going on to high school. The final three years (usually between ages 15 and 18) they attend "lycee" (high school); they are required to have a specialization upon graduation which is stated on their diploma. Upon graduating from high school in France, their education is equivalent to approximately that of a two-year degree (associate degree) from an American school. The grading scale used in schools goes from 1 to 20 with 1 being the lowest grade and 20 being the highest grade. The rigor of the high school curriculum requires diligence; it is not uncommon for students to drop out before obtaining their diploma.

Since the school where I was teaching was a "college" (middle school), I taught classes ranging in age from 11 to 15 years old. The grades at a college were called the 6e (6th grade), 5e (7th grade), 4e (8th grade), and 3e (9th grade).

My teaching duties began with meeting the six English teachers and observing their classes. I found that one of the teachers, Madame Ruffaut, had been an exchange teacher in Columbia, South Carolina, about twenty-five years earlier. Since there were several classes of each level, I spent two to three weeks observing classes as the teachers determined the most appropriate days for me to visit. I was very eager to see the English textbooks and observe how my native language was taught. I found that the teachers used a combination of textbook and audio material. In addition to the exercises they had in class and for homework from the textbook, the teachers had them listen to audio recordings of native English speakers and would have them answer written questions about what they heard or would ask them questions. The English used in these materials was primarily British English. Lessons were a combination of grammar, reading, comprehension, conversation, and some cultural tidbits. Students usually began studying foreign languages in their first year (6e) at the "college." English, considered a universal language, was the most popular language followed by German and Spanish because of the close proximity of the countries of Germany and Spain to France. Other languages taught were Italian and Latin, since Italy shared a border with France and Latin was useful in learning vocabulary.

France is approximately the size of the state of Texas and is one of the larger West European countries. Because of its size and proximity to countries of different languages, its inhabitants are very likely to encounter and communicate with persons from other countries. In contrast, the size of the United States and its physical isolation on both the east and west sides by oceans caused many Americans to view learning a foreign language as a luxury during the 1980s. However, the increasing globalization of the world by the Internet and influx of more foreigners during the 1990s have dramatically changed this view.

The first class I observed was Madame Moulin's class which was a class of 3e (15 year olds). Most of them were in their fourth year of studying English so Madame Moulin had them ask me questions to get them to use their English and become acquainted with me. They asked questions such as: What is your name? Where are you from? How long have you been here? What do you do? How many brothers and sisters have you got? Where do your parents live? What are your hobbies? I asked them some of the same questions. Some were too shy or nervous since I was a native speaker, but several piped up without hesitation. One of the first things that they and I noticed was the difference in the American English I spoke and the British English they had learned. When I asked them about their family, I would say "How many brothers and sisters *do you hav*e?" whereas they would ask me 'How many brothers and sisters *have you got*?' They immediately looked to their teacher for an explanation of this difference, and she explained that the difference was due to the fact that the American and British English sometimes differed in the way things were phrased and gave them other examples of differences.

At the end of October, I had spent about eight to twelve hours per week observing six to eight classes and becoming acquainted with the teachers and students. The teachers then decided which students would benefit most from my conversation and cultural classes and decided to either send some advanced students for me to teach during their normal class periods, let the students come voluntarily during part of their lunch break, or have me come to their class and involve the students in question and dialogue as it pertained to the lesson.

When I went to one of the 11-year-old classes (6e), some of the students immediately called me "Monsieur Chocolat" (Mr. Chocolate) since they had had little contact with black persons. I had wondered for quite a while about the population of native blacks and noticed that I only saw blacks who seemed to be French early in the morning performing such tasks as street sweepers or hotel maids. Most of the other blacks I saw were students from Africa.

Being a black American piqued most of their curiosity and during my first class with some of the 14 and 15 year olds who came during their lunch period, I divided them into groups and gave them pictures of my immediate family, parents, and grandparents for them to discuss among themselves and prepare questions for me.

After questioning me about the age of my parents and siblings and where they lived, they asked me how long I had lived in America. When I responded that I was born there, they asked me how long my parents had lived there, when my grandparents came to America and if they had been slaves. I soon learned that even though they had seen blacks in American movies, were fans of some black musicians and singers such as Ray Charles and Stevie Wonder, told me about several black actors and actresses, and adored Michael Jackson that they basically thought of America as being white. Their perception of America was based on the Americans they saw in movies, and they rarely saw blacks except in entertainment or in sports. They adored America and exhibited no prejudice toward me as a black American but were surprised to know that the population of blacks in America was as large as it was and that blacks were involved in all arenas of American society.

After being at the school for a month, I realized that of all the students and teachers, I was the only black in the school. However, because I felt so welcomed, I rarely thought of it. In the second part of the school year, a student arrived from one of the African francophone countries which was fighting a civil war; she spoke French and was immediately befriended by the students.

Several years after I returned to the United States, I began studying black American history in depth and found that during the latter part of the nineteenth century and much of the twentieth century, many black Americans in various fields left the United States and came to France to study or live because of the oppression and denial of opportunity before the passage of the Civil Rights laws in the 1960s. A few which come to mind immediately are Ernest Everett Just, an international marine biologist; Norbert Rillieux, the inventor of the sugar evaporating pan; Bessie Coleman, the first black female aviator; James Baldwin, a well-known writer; Henry O'Tanner, an international artist; and Julian Abele, the architect who designed the Duke Chapel at Duke University.

Mahalia Jackson, the queen of black gospel music from the 1940s until her death in 1972, constantly butted heads with segregation and discrimination in the South during the 1950s and 1960s even though she was a very successful singer. However, she went on a singing tour in Europe in the 1950s and was hailed and loved so much that America decided to embrace her as one of its own. Before my in-depth study of black history, I had no idea that the French knew who she was until I heard one of her albums playing as I was descending the stairs in my hotel one day. I stopped two or three times and thought that I was hearing the singing in my head. My landlord and landlady were Caucasian, and even though they seemed to be very knowledgeable of American culture I found it unbelievable that I was hearing black gospel music coming from their apartment on the third floor. That evening when most of us were in the lounge recounting the day's activities as we waited for the evening news to come on, I asked Madame Caron if I did indeed hear her playing a song by Mahalia Jackson. Her eyes and mouth immediately flew open with raving admiration. *"OH OUI!! Elle est magnifique!! Quelle voix!!! Je l'adore!!!"* (OH YES!! She is magnificent!! What a voice!! I adore her!!!) she exclaimed. I was shocked! I was still thinking that I had heard Mahalia singing in my head, because I missed hearing gospel music and the church services to which I was accustomed. I had brought lots of cassettes with me but missed being in the church services at home.

Some of the students had heard and wanted to know if it was true that there were actually segregated neighborhoods in America and the reason for this if it was true. It shocked them to learn that black and white neighborhoods still existed even though legal segregation had ended; they thought of America as a progressive country where equal opportunity existed not only in the law but in the minds of most of its people.

This is not to imply that France has had a perfect past or that prejudice or racism doesn't exist in France, because it does but is not between blacks and whites but is usually between Caucasians and Arabs. The war between France and Algeria which ended in 1962 with Algerian independence from France left bitter feelings between the two countries and persons of Arab descent. However, I must also admit that blacks from Africa did not always feel the same warmth that black Americans felt since America was regarded as the golden land flowing with opportunity and wealth. Many students and some teachers thought that almost all Americans were wealthy.

Even though they had some misconceptions about America, the students were well informed about American entertainment. Since I had been raised without television, most of the students knew more about Americans in entertainment than I did and imitated some of the things in class they had seen in American movies. However, not only were the teenagers very knowledgeable about American entertainers but also most of the teachers and other adults. The adults loved former President John F. Kennedy and usually cited him as their favorite president, knew generally how American politics worked, and were quite knowledgeable of the geography of the United States. When asked to name the states in the United States, the ones that came to students' minds quickly were New York, California, Texas, and Florida. Just as many Americans only think of Paris when they think of France, many French only think of New York when they think of America. To help them become more familiar with other states, I had them fill in a map of the states in America and told them bits of information about several states. Most thought that North and South Carolina were one state. Many of them wanted to visit the Statue of Liberty, the White House, the Grand Canyon, and Disney World.

Teaching was really fun with basically no stress since I had no papers to grade nor gave grades. Once while I was teaching some of the 5e (seventh grade equivalent), I turned my back to the class to write on the board and found spitballs hitting the board as I wrote. Well, I thought to myself, so they do that over here too – just like some of my former classmates in America. And, just as in the United States, this age group proved to be the most active and mischievous of all the age groups I taught since they were between childhood and adolescence and often misbehaved to push the limits or amuse their classmates.

I mainly supplemented what the students learned in their classes and gave them a chance to perform real life situations. To simulate shopping in America, I divided them in groups, gave them sales papers from department and grocery stores in the United States, gave them American money, and had them buy presents for their families and grocery items; I acted as the cashier but they had to verify that I had charged them correctly and given them the correct change. This exercise forced them to use the vocabulary they had learned in their English classes, learn new vocabulary, compare clothing sizes with those in France, and become more familiar with American money.

In November, we did a lesson on Thanksgiving and sang a turkey song which included a phrase that said "Gobble, gobble, gobble." They liked the song, but really loved saying "gobble, gobble, gobble" and went to their other classes singing. This helped them with their pronunciation of the American short 'o' sound since they tended to pronounce the 'o' as they pronounce it in their language which is equivalent to the 'o' sound in the word *love* in our language. It was odd not observing Thanksgiving while there since this holiday does not exist in France. After I returned to the United States, some of the students would write me and end their letters with "Gobble, gobble, Mr. James."

I also did other lessons that corresponded with holidays or special events. This gave me an opportunity not only to expose them to American culture but also to learn more about their culture as they explained their traditions and how they celebrated certain holidays or events. We talked about the traditions and foods associated with holidays such as Christmas, New Year's, Valentine's Day, and Easter. In addition, we discussed the American school system and compared it to the French school system and briefly discussed black history month and religion. While discussing religion, I gave them examples of Biblical English and compared it to modern English and played church songs to see how much of the song they understood before giving them the words of the song. They were quite thrilled with the lively rhythm of some of the music as they clapped and told me that it was very different from the solemn music they heard at their churches. A few years after I returned to Chapel Hill, I met a group of students from France at UNC-Chapel Hill who requested to be taken to a lively black church. I inquired as to how they knew about the music and singing characteristic of black churches, and they informed me that they had seen it on television in France.

Two classes were outstanding in their attendance and interest; most of the students from these classes never missed even though they came voluntarily during hours assigned by their teachers or during the latter half of their lunch period which lasted one and a half to two hours. One of these classes had a mixture of students in the 3e and 4e levels. One student, Claire Gouget, became my sister's pen pal. After she finished high school, she went to a Canadian university in Montreal and later invited me and my sister to her wedding there and also drove to North Carolina once with her aunt, uncle, and cousin to meet my mother and two sisters who drove up from South Carolina.

Former student Claire Gouget (left) and her husband, Benoit (right), on their wedding day (July 1993) in Montreal, Canada, with me and my sister, Cynthia.

Other students such as Donia Ayari, Olivia Barthomeuf, Ounassa Aoubid, and Francois Gay continued to write me years after I had left and some still write informing me of their travels and occupations. About seven to ten students in Madame Moulin's class were highly motivated and we did an enactment of *Jack and the Beanstalk* which another English teach, Monsieur Soucheyre, videotaped and filed in the school's library.

Lunchtime was one of the daily highlights at the school. I usually ate lunch at the school, because the food was usually quite good and inexpensive. The teachers sat together and the students sat with their classes and were monitored by members of the school staff. The French baguette and table wine were staple items which were served daily; wine was only available at the teachers' table. Lunch was served family style to the teachers and students and brought to the table in courses just as it was in homes. The first course usually consisted of a salad or raw vegetables followed by a meat and side dish. Next, cheese was served and then some fruit and/or dessert. As I mentioned beforehand, cheese is served at lunch and dinner with most French meals, because it is such an integral part of French cuisine. France produces more than 400 kinds of cheeses. Each region of France is known for a different type of cheese; the type and flavor of cheese is determined by the animal which produces it, the land, and the climate. In fact, ripening cheese so that it attains its best flavor before being sold is an artistic occupation in France.

Lunch gave me a chance to taste a wide variety of French cuisine and to eat some things I never would have eaten in America if I was not truly hungry. One of those things was beef tongue. When I saw it on the menu one week, I had no desire for it but by lunchtime on the day it was served I was so hungry that I had a slight headache. So even though it had a funny and slightly coarse texture, I had a second serving of it. However, I have not eaten it since my return to the United States and have had no taste for it. One dish that I found delicious was potato pie, not sweet potato pie (I rarely saw sweet potatoes in France) but white potato pie which was encrusted top and bottom and was slightly enriched with a white creamy potato sauce. I craved it from time to time after leaving France.

Teachers at the school lunch table

Note: On the following page is one of the school lunch menus. Translation is given on the succeeding page. Lunch was not served on the Mondays shown because school was out; the French have many more days off from school than Americans. In addition, lunch was not served on Wednesdays because they were half-days on the dates shown. However, lunch was served on Saturdays which were usually half-days.

Collège LES CELESTINS
03200 VICHY

MENU

DU _09 au 13 Mai_
ET
DU _16 au 20 Mai_

LUNDI		LUNDI	
MARDI 9	Radis. Saucisson. Beurre Poisson pané sauce tomate Pates Orange	MARDI 16	Salade aux oeufs durs Raviolis gratinés Fromage blanc Pomme
MERCREDI 10		MERCREDI 17	
JEUDI 11	Salade Poule au riz sauce suprême Pâtisserie	JEUDI 18	Crudités Roti de porc sauce tartare Lentilles Fruits au sirop. Biscuit.
VENDREDI 12	Tomates. Thon en salade Rosbeef Frites Tartare. Pomme	VENDREDI 19	Macédoine. Tomates Saumonnette mayonnaise Pommes boulangères Six de Savoie. Orange
SAMEDI 13	Salade d'endives Escalopes panées Petits pois Banane	SAMEDI 20	Oeufs mimosa Beef hachés Haricots panachés Yaourts

Le Gestionnaire,   Le Principal,

MENU

From May 9 – 13

And

From May 16 – 20

Monday	Monday
Tuesday (9th)	Tuesday (16th)
Radish. Sausage. Butter	Salad w/hard-boiled eggs
Fish w/bread crumbs in tomato sauce	Ravioli sprinkled w/browned cheese
Pastries	White cheese
Orange	Apple
Wednesday (10th)	Wednesday (17th)
Thursday (11th)	Thursday (18th)
Salad	Raw vegetables
Chicken w/rice and supreme sauce	Roasted pork w/mayonnaise
Cake	Lentils
	Fruit cocktail. Cookie
Friday (12th)	Friday (19th)
Tomatoes. Tuna Salad	Diced vegetables. Tomatoes
Roast beef	Salmon w/mayonnaise
Fries	Baked apples
Sauce. Apple	Six de Savoie (Brand of cookies).
Orange	
Saturday (13th)	Saturday (20th)
Endive salad	Mimosa eggs
Cutlet (veal) w/bread crumbs	Chopped beef
Green peas	Assorted beans
Banana	Yogurt

The Administrator   The Principal

I not only tasted much of the French cuisine but also got to know and converse with teachers who taught other subjects. The life of the table was Mademoiselle Danielle Favory, a history and geography teacher who truly enjoyed teaching and had traveled throughout France and taken trips to many other countries including three or more trips to different parts of the United States. Everyday when she entered the cafeteria, she asked me "How are yoouuuuu?" This always brought a chuckle from the other teachers; she was always jovial and was at ease with everyone. She told me that she had tried her best to learn English while in school but had a bad teacher and thus quit trying. Now since she was middle-aged, she said she was too old to learn it but could ask simple questions and say "Excuse me, please." During my first month, she would ask if everything was going all right and if everyone was treating me well. One day she told the other teachers that she had seen a picture in one of the local newspapers of the orientation in Clermont-Ferrand of all the English and Spanish teachers from abroad and that I was seated on the front row. When no one else said they had seen it, she brought the article to lunch a few days later and brought me the picture which she had gotten from the newspaper office. This is the picture at the beginning of this chapter. I thanked her greatly for her kindness; she was always bringing things of interest to the lunch table for someone which created a pleasant atmosphere.

Even though she was jovial, she was honest about the history of France and its current problems. In fact, she informed me that Vichy had been the seat of the Nazis in France during World War II. The only time I saw her slightly upset was when some of the English teachers planned a trip for the students to Great Britain without consulting the other teachers. She had already planned a trip for her history or geography class which involved many of the same students and had to cancel the trip. Because of this, she called some of the English teachers *andouilles* (sausages) which meant they had bad upbringing in not having the courtesy to consult with their colleagues before making such plans. This was a new vocabulary word for me. I felt somewhat bad about this since some of the English teachers later invited me to go on this five to seven day trip with them and the students free of charge the last week of June. My contract with the school ended in May and I'd have to stay an extra month. However, I consented to going as I would only have to take spending money.

Unfortunately, about a month prior to the trip when I phoned the airlines to see how soon I could return to the United States after the trip, I was told that since I had an open book ticket that I would have to wait until August if I did not return in June. It was vacation season and all planes from France to all destinations in the United States were fully booked for the month of July and much of August. My funds would not last that long, so I had to forego the trip to Britain and return in June.

One of the things that amazed me was the amount of breaks in the school calendar. Classes seldom went five weeks without breaking for a week or a few days. I had no complaints about this since it gave me time to take short trips and do lots of reading. This idea of taking time to relax and enjoy life is part of the French culture and even permeates the workplace where most employers grant workers five weeks of vacation when they become employed; they may accumulate more weeks as their time of employment with the company or agency increases. I thus felt a lot less stressed than I would have in the United States. During one of these breaks, I went

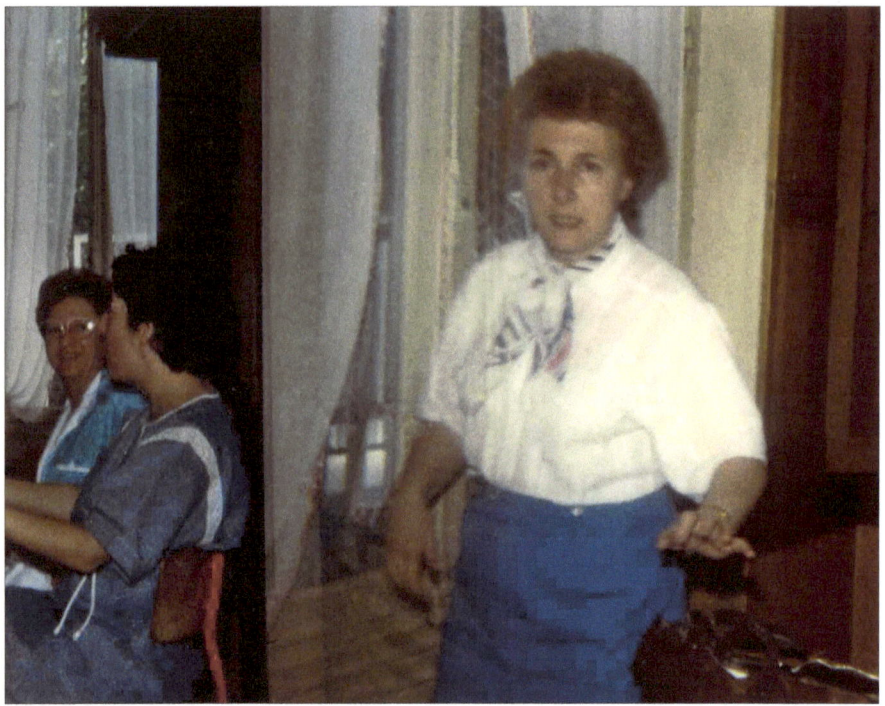

Left: Music teacher and an office administrator talk over lunch.
Right: Mlle Danielle Favory (the life of the lunch table) grabs her belongings before leaving the lunch room.

cross-country skiing with some of the faculty and students. It was my first time skiing and I fell rather frequently at first but soon got the hang of it and did fairly well though I did not try speeding down any slopes. After two to three hours I came to the end of the trail; it was quite a workout and I welcomed the hot chocolate served to us in the refreshment building. The next day, my muscles let me know that they had been exerted.

In the spring, I took a field trip to Paris by train with one of the history classes. It was 1989 - the bicentennial of the French Revolution and the centennial of the Eiffel Tower. The main purpose of the trip was to attend a drama featuring some of the key figures from the revolution who wore attire from the era and gave speeches from many of those living during that period. Afterwards, we toured the city briefly and had lunch by the Eiffel Tower.

Thus, teaching the students and interacting with the teachers enlivened my experience and opened the door for friendships. Apart from the students being more knowledgeable of people and events outside their country than most Americans, they were much like American students.

Cross-country skiing with some of my students

Left and below: 5e students (7th grade equivalent) socialize and play during their lunch break.

Note: On the opposite page is a copy of the certificate awarded to me by the school at the end of the academic year.

CERTIFICAT

M. *JAMES Walter*

Nationalité : *Américaine*

a exercé les fonctions d'assistant du *1.10.1988* au *31.05.89*

NOM de l'établissement : *Collège Mixte "Les Célestins". 125, rue Maréchal Lyautey 03200 VICHY*

Académie de *CLERMONT-FERRAND*

Date : *31 mai 1989*   Signature :

Qualité du signataire
et cachet de l'établissement

J. SOULIS
Principal

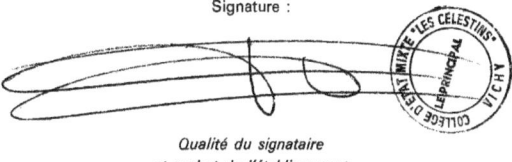

Cette attestation sera remise à l'assistant(e) au moment de son départ ou envoyée directement à l'intéressé(e) par l'établissement. Aucun duplicata ne pourra en être fourni ultérieurement.

Chapter Twelve – French Friendships

What is friendship? What would cause you to consider someone as your friend? For many Americans, a friend could be someone they know casually, have known for years, or have just met a few minutes ago. They may have had deep discussions with the person and know the inner feelings of the individual, or they may have had casual conversations with the individual but not know the individual's feelings on matters they deem important. They may keep in contact with the person if they live nearby or touch bases on a regular basis if they live far apart. Or, they may stop communicating with the individual if the person moves to another city or state but would make time to get together if one or the other visited the city where the other was living.

For many Americans, however, friendship is superficial. Two people often call each other friends and know little about the other's soul – that is, their heartfelt feelings, emotions, achievements, dreams, disappointments, backgrounds, and views on life and the events and experiences that have molded the other's life or determined the other's outlook on life. Few persons maintain communication with a friend who has moved to another city or another state. And to maintain ties with a friend who has moved to another country is even more unlikely. The Internet and e-mail have made this easier in the 1990s and twenty-first century, but Americans in general treat friendship as superfluous. As our lives accelerate to keep pace with instant technology, the value and loyalty of human relationships decelerate with the accumulation of gadget materialism.

In France, however, and in my interaction with persons of other nationalities I have often found higher esteem and value placed on relationships than materialism. One of the most admirable things I learned firsthand about the French was the quality of their friendships. In America, friends are easily made and sometimes just as easily discarded. In France, however, friends are harder to make but much more likely to be retained even after years of geographical separation. In America, you may be invited to someone's home after meeting the person briefly if the two of you had a sense of camaraderie when you first talked. In France, one is usually not invited to another's home until one has known and talked with the invitee several times for a few months. An invitation to someone's home (without accompaniment of another party already known by the individual who invites you) is a serious gesture of friendship in France. It is an invitation to walk through a door that will likely remain open for a lifetime if one is apt at maintaining communication beyond a few weeks or months.

After being at the school for several weeks, I was invited by the assistant math teacher to have dinner with him and his friends one Saturday in Clermont-Ferrand. He was from Morocco and was there to teach math for a year while he was studying. His friends were students in Clermont-Ferrand, if I remember correctly. Upon arriving at their apartment, I was greeted by the smell of meat and vegetables cooking. They were very generous in serving and I tasted couscous (small rice-like grain) for the first time which they served with beef and nicely seasoned carrots, beans, and other chopped vegetables. It was delicious and I had two servings. They spoke fairly fluent French which was the second official language in their country and told me about the customs and educational system in Morocco. After spending several hours with them, I boarded the train back to Vichy.

I spent Christmas alone but was invited to Madame Moulin's (one of the English teachers) home for New Year's. Here I got a very good cultural introduction to the French way of celebrating the New Year (See journal entry in appendix dated Dec. 31 – Jan. 1).

After a few months I was also invited to the home of another teacher, Madame Therre, whose son, Alexandre Therre, was in one of my 4e classes (8th grade equivalent). Monsieur Therre, her husband, taught at a nearby *lycee* (high school) and was very knowledgeable of the history of the different regions of France and the entire country. I went to their home twice and enjoyed delicious home cooked dinners and engaging discussions on both occasions. Not only did they invite me into their home, but Monsieur Therre and Alexandre took me on two tours to different towns within a hour or so of Vichy where Monsieur Therre stopped and pointed out signs and different historic points within the towns and along the way. One of the places we visited was the site (near Lignon) where the French novel *L'Astree* occurred; this was the first novel I studied in the first graduate literature course I took at UNC-Chapel Hill. Details of the novel were fresh in my head because of the comical manner in which Dr. George B. Daniel taught the novel in my seventeenth century literature class. I was very grateful to Monsieur Therre for taking the time to be such an excellent tour guide on these two excursions. Monsieur and Madame Therre and their son Alexandre still write me every year around Christmas. Alexandre now has an administrative position in a hospital near Paris.

In addition, I still correspond with the librarian, Mademoiselle Arlette Janiaud; Mademoiselle Danielle Favory; and Madame Moulin, all of whom are now retired.

Alexandre Therre (student) and myself at the site of the French novel, *L'Astree*, on excursion led by his father.

Chapter Thirteen – Other Excursions in France

In addition to going on field trips with classes and the excursions I made as a guest of the Therre family, I also went on two or three one and two hour trips on Sunday afternoons with three to four retired teachers whom I met through Hazel, the English teacher assistant from England who resided at the hotel where I stayed. She had met these teachers through someone at the *lycee* where she taught and asked them if I could come along. Being educators they were very good informants and often planned the trips to visit chateaus or the ruins of chateaus. It seemed that the region where I resided had more chateaus than any other region in France. The teachers were all very cordial and pleasant. We usually stopped at some place to have a patisserie and/or coffee or hot chocolate. They usually took two cars so everyone could travel comfortably; touring France by car with personal tour guides who were educators was the most enjoyable means of discovering the towns and villages.

On excursion with retired teachers visiting the ruins of the *chateau d'Urfe* in the department of *Loire*. From left to right are: Monsieur Aubert, English teacher; Monsieur Depalle, primary school teacher; myself; and Mademoiselle LaCroix – Greek, Latin, and French teacher.

I soon understood what the French meant when they said that almost every town and city in America were basically the same in appearance, because in the United States we usually find basically the same kinds of stores or franchises in most places we visit. In France, however, almost every town or village had its own flavor which often reflected its history by the names of different places and streets and the types of material from which some of the buildings had been constructed. In addition, each region was known for its cuisine specialty which was reflected in the types of cheese or grapes produced from the land as well as certain traditional dishes.

The only major trip that I took alone was to Melun, a small town south of Paris, to see the chateau Vaux-le-Vicomte. I traveled by train and had to go north to Paris first and then switch trains for a 20-minute or so ride south to the town. I was first introduced to the history of this chateau by Dr. Joseph James, my undergraduate French professor, at Francis Marion College in Florence, South Carolina, and was intrigued not only by its history but also by the beautiful pictures I had seen of it. It was built by Nicolas Fouquet, the finance minister of Louis XIV (the king), in 1661.

It was an eloquent structure with elaborate decorations and gardens with the shrubs and other plants trimmed in circular patterns characteristic of the baroque period in France. Upon completion of the chateau and its grounds, Nicolas threw a grand party to which he invited Louis XIV in addition to other persons of royal esteem. He gave expensive prizes to the men and women who attended. Louis XIV was overcome with jealousy and accused Nicolas of embezzlement, had him imprisoned, and took the architect, gardener, painter and decorator and cook of the palace to construct and serve at Versailles (a palace for him). His intent was to build a more beautiful place than Vaux-le-Vicomte. However, to date, many persons find Vaux-le-Vicomte and its gardens with its baroque style of circular patterns more beautiful than Versailles whose gardens were built in a classical style with linear designs.

From the train station, I had to take a taxi to the chateau which was quite expensive. However, I felt that my visit to the chateau was worth the cost; it was one of the sites I was determined to see during my stay in France this time because of its historical significance.

Chapter Fourteen – Other Experiences and Observations

France is known for its cuisine and I found its food to be quite tasty. One of my favorite places to go in my neighborhood was the *patisserie* which I visited two to three times weekly to get one or two delicacies which were baked daily. I sometimes bought a baguette and had to get used to carrying it down the street with only a small piece of paper wrapped around it. At first it seemed unsanitary, but I soon thought little of it.

I also enjoyed eating fish with rice in the school cafeteria and in a few homes that I visited. I had almost stopped eating fish in the United States unless it was salmon or already prepared in some special manner; the smell of fish frying had once stayed with me for almost a week as a child and turned my appetite. However, the manner in which fish was prepared with rice here lured my taste buds.

Another dish I enjoyed which was rich and rather heavy to the stomach was a dessert pie called the *galette des rois* which was served in January in the school cafeteria on the day that the wise men supposedly came to visit the Christ child.

One American dish that I really missed and never saw was macaroni and cheese. Macaroni was fairly common in salads and other dishes but was never served with cheese. I once attempted to make some in my apartment, but could not find any French cheese with the right consistency. I also missed the abundance of ice in drinks when eating in restaurants and in some homes. Most restaurants serve Coke or other drinks with two or three small cubes of ice per glass so that the drink is cool at best and never ice cold as we are accustomed to in the United States.

Another thing that was different was the color of the cars' headlights; they were yellow. Also, the French were not as concerned with the care of their cars as Americans were; they would drive up on the curb or sidewalk without hesitation to maneuver into a parking space. I often had to watch out for cars coming up on the sidewalk while I was walking. Another interesting thing was that the trains rarely blew their whistles; they blew them to announce departures from a major station or if they saw the potential for an accident but not as they approached street intersections. However, almost all intersections had warning lights and/or crossbars. Whistle blowing had been banned to reduce noise pollution.

Since my stay lasted from September to June and my previous stay was in June and July, I experienced all four seasons which were basically the same as in North Carolina except that warm weather was not definite until June. It snowed once or twice during the winter but did not snow enough to cover the ground. By April we were having warm days, the flowers were blooming, and the trees were budding, but I was informed that the inconsistency in warm and cold temperatures usually lasted until May. However, the inconsistency lasted longer this year. In fact, on the day that I boarded the train for my trip back to the United States near the end of June, I had to wear a jacket because there was enough chill in the air and had been during the week for people to turn their heaters back on. Even though a cool day in the early summer was not unusual, almost everyone was surprised that it was cold enough to turn on their heaters.

As I mentioned in a previous chapter, I was somewhat surprised at the number of breaks we got from school during the year. I adapted to this with little difficulty but had more difficulty in adjusting to the number of labor strikes. It seemed that some group or persons representing some occupation were always on strike. Usually the strikes involved government employees in transportation, hospitals, or the postal service demanding higher pay and better benefits. During the strikes, only essential services were available from these agencies. Everyone was affected by the postal workers but the French seemed to take it in stride as part of the work culture. The postal workers went on strike three to four times during my second stay; one strike lasted over a month. This was wearisome to me since I looked forward to receiving letters and cards from my friends and family in the United States. Events such as these made me more appreciative of the dependability of such services in America where strikes are much less common.

I went to the post office quite frequently and had one experience which somewhat frightened me as I was walking there (downtown) one day. Several blocks from the post office, I realized that I was being followed by two Caucasian teenagers who appeared to be between 14 and 16 years old. Since I had been in Vichy for several months and recognized many of the students from the school when I saw them on the street, I sensed that these two boys were not from Vichy and didn't seem to be heading in a definite direction. Although the streets were busy as usual, I felt somewhat afraid and quickened my pace. I thought of being kidnapped and held as an American hostage even though this was unlikely in such a small city. However, the recent bombing of the Pan Am airline by Libya and a few other terrorist activities in other countries was on my mind, and I wondered if some terrorist had these two boys following me to stop me with innocent questions to ascertain my identity as an

American and then suddenly kidnap me. The boys continued following me to the post office where I thought they would either disappear or wait outside once I entered federal premises. I decided that if I saw them when I came back outside that I would return inside and ask one of the postal employees what I should do since I was obviously being followed by strangers. To my surprise, they came inside and waited by the door as I went to one of the postal clerks to mail the postcards I had with me.

There were several entrance and exit doors to the post office, but I decided to go to the door where they were standing; I was going to find out then and there what they were up to and if there was trouble I figured the best place to handle it would be in a federal building with federal employees present. As I approached them, they were smiling. I spoke first with the French greeting of '*Bonjour*'; they returned the greeting. Speaking totally in French I asked them how they were and if I could help them. At this, they struggled to speak French but spoke mostly English. Sensing that they were not French and unable to tell by their English accent what country they might be from, I asked them the same questions in broken English (pretending that I could not speak English well and didn't totally understand it). My purpose was not to let them know that I was American.

When I began speaking English, they told me that they were from Australia and were traveling with a soccer team. They had been allowed some free time to do a little sightseeing and get some lunch and were looking for someone who could speak English to direct them to a good but inexpensive restaurant. Upon hearing this I was relieved and let my guard down and began to speak English freely. I walked with them to a restaurant while talking with them and found that their team was touring and competing in soccer matches in several countries across Europe. The more we talked the more comfortable I felt and let them know that I was from the United States at which they expressed no surprise. I agreed to have lunch with them once we arrived at the restaurant and translated several items on the menu for them so they would have a better chance of choosing something they liked. We continued to talk as we were served, and they asked me what I was doing in Vichy, if I had visited Paris, what part of the United States I was from and what I was studying. I then had to ask the question that was still on my mind: What caused them to think I could speak English just from seeing me on the street? I was both curious and wondered if I stood out as an American target. They said they just had a feeling that I could and took the chance of asking me since they needed someone to point them to a reasonable restaurant. I enjoyed their company and parted with them upon leaving the restaurant.

That evening as we gathered in the lounge at the hotel, I told some of the others and Madame Caron, the landlady, of my experience and was still surprised that someone would follow me to the post office and wait by the door to see if I could speak English so they could find a reasonably priced restaurant. Madame Caron didn't seem surprised. She said that I didn't stand out as an American, but that they probably thought I could speak English since I was black and most blacks in France were from Africa and could speak English. In addition, she stated that I probably seemed easy to approach. This all seemed logical but still amazed me. Later when I told someone about the experience after returning to the United States, they asked me if I was wearing white tennis shoes to which I responded positively. They then pointed out that my white tennis shoes (sneakers) probably gave me away as an

American. In most other countries, tennis shoes are black, blue, or some other color; Americans can often be spotted overseas since they are usually the only ones with white tennis shoes. This now made total sense to me. Being in sports and traveling to different countries, I'm sure that they were aware of the different types of sports shoes worn in different countries and thus would have assumed that I was American and thus spoke English because of my shoes. Well, I'll know next time.

Chapter Fifteen – The Change in Me

As one would expect, my level of confidence in transacting daily business and traveling was even higher than at the end of my first stay in Vichy. I felt that I could move to a larger city in France and have no real problem looking out for myself and doing daily tasks and errands.

I was also aware of changes within myself – I had spoken French daily for so long that I had actually forgotten the English words for some objects like china closet, chest of drawers, and other pieces of furniture. I could only refer to them by their French names. I also noticed that I was slightly more aggressive when performing errands such as exchanging money at the bank or requesting a student discount for a ticket at the train station. I had come to realize that it was the French way to say they couldn't perform a transaction or was unaware that a discount was available but would give in and do so when you were aggressive or pressed the issue and realized you knew what you were talking about or if you let them know that you had seen them do it before for someone else.

The nine months also helped me to realize what part of me was really me and what part of me was just American culture or my reaction to being raised in American society. For example, I found that I not only enjoyed meeting foreigners when I was in America but also felt at ease living among them. My personality was still basically that of an introvert but I found I opened up more once I found I didn't have to be constantly on guard for fear of my actions being judged according to my race. However, I was still aware of racism directed toward other ethnics and felt for them. I was willing to try different foods but as was typical of me, I never threw caution to the wind and tried something when I had no idea of what it was.

Upon my return to the United States, others also noticed that I had changed. Once again, I had lost weight but not as much as I had during my previous stay. This time I had had more control over my menu and my appetite was better since dogs were not inside my residence. However, I had picked up the habit of laying my bread directly on the table beside my plate when I sat down to eat and was not even aware of it until someone called my attention to it. I had never done this before my trips to France but had picked it up since most French meals are begun by placing bread on the table. One usually gets a piece of bread and place it on the table beside the plate to have it available for sopping the plate after each course is served. My English accent was also different; my pronunciation of English words was more precise for several weeks after my return, since I had to pronounce English words very clearly when teaching.

However, the biggest change that those around me daily noticed was the increased speed at which I expressed disagreement and requested others to prove their points during conversation. Whereas I had been very calm and would either shrug off disagreement by not saying anything or only state my view and one or two opposing examples even if I was sure that I was correct, I would now let the individual know firmly that I disagreed with their point of view, state my view with supporting facts or examples, and ask the opposing individual to do the same for their view and not allow them to abandon the subject until they had done so if they continued to press the issue. This caused some of my friends to take a few steps back from me since they had never seen me be aggressive, even though I was not the initiator of the debate. I then became conscious of the change and tried to tone down a bit since I had no desire to be or appear contentious. Being in the French environment where conversations could easily turn to debate to prove a point or just for the sake of debating and where most did not hesitate to express their feelings and where I had been forced to sometimes argue with persons during transactions at the bank, train station, etc. had made me more aggressive and quicker to express disagreement. Even today though I always try to be objective and have facts before I object to or express disagreement about something, it is difficult for me to shrug something off or passively ignore something when I feel that it is wrong and adversely affects someone.

In addition to the changes within me, I also had more confidence in teaching when I returned to UNC-Chapel Hill that fall to teach intermediate French and further my studies. My experiences and additional materials used in everyday life for visual aids and hands-on exercises enlivened my classes and gave them a better grasp of the language and culture.

I have not yet returned to France but still communicate with the teachers and students I met there via letters, cards, and e-mails. When I visit again, it will be great to know that time and space have not separated us nor suffered or broken our friendship.

Appendix

Welcome Letter from School Administrator (Mme Feuillat) in Vichy

Dec. 31, 1988 – Jan. 1, 1989 - New Year's celebration at Mme Moulin's home

Feb. 26, 1989 – Excursion to Volvic and Riom

April 7, 1989 – Excursion to Thiers

May 15, 1989 – Excursion to Boen

Collège d'Etat Mixte
LES CELESTINS
125, rue du Ml-Lyautey
03200 VICHY

Vichy, le 16 juin 1988.

Dear Mister James,

We are informed of your nomination as an assistant in English at our college.

It will be the first time to us to welcome a student coming from the United State of Illinois. For details, you may write to Miss J.T. Heather, 45, Burleigh Road, Ipswich - Suffolk, IP4 5LJ, England.

In our school, you'll meet and work with girls and boys from 11 to 15 years old.

Vichy is a well-known watering place with a romantic charm dating from the 19th century like that of your old Carolina. But it is also a modern town with clubs, library, swimming, tennis courts and all kind of sports.

you'll have your lunch, only if you like, in our dining-room (at a low price) with the other teachers. Then the Matron will lead you in their very friendly house and will, with permission of our City's Mayor, place to your disposal very near our notices.

When you'll know the date of your arrival, please, let us know and will be at the station to bring you to your residence.

Sincerely yours

J. Feuillat

Dec. 31, 1988 - Jan. 1, 1989

After having dinner w/ Mme Moulin's family on Dec. 27, 1988, I was invited to pass from the Old Year to the New Year with them on the evening of Dec. 31. I agreed heartily as I had enjoyed meeting & eating w/her family on Dec. 27. Mme Moulin picked me up at 6pm at my residence (Hôtel des Victoires), and we headed for her home in Cusset which is approximately 6km outside of Vichy (her home, that is). They live on the edge of the country in a very nice house (she, her husband, three children - 1 girl & 2 boys, and one neat cat). Stopped to get gas just before turning on one of the last roads leading to her house. Got to house. Her husband's mother and two brothers were there along with the second brother's wife. The youngest brother's wife had decided to pass the holiday w/her parents because she had recently learned that her father had cancer. The brother's kids were there also. I sat down by the fireplace & had a short discussion w/ Mme Moulin's husband on the educational system in France. Afterwards I and his next oldest brother got into a discussion on the geography of the U.S. & other interesting facts about the U.S. Soon we started talking about England. Mme Moulin, her mother-in-law, and this brother's wife soon joined us. I asked Mme Moulin one question about the English schools and she started talking faster than a radio. She speaks fast but clearly. That's one thing that tickles me; no matter where I go I find that the women can really add fuel to a conversation. Once they start talking, it's like unleashing water that's been held back by a dam. Soon she told me to come into the kitchen

2

and watch the men at work. What were they doing? Opening up oysters! There must have been about 200 or more oysters there. Of course they were still alive & you could see them moving their tiny "feet" when their shells were opened. I looked closely at one of them, and I beheld a little red worm crawling out one of the shells. They had not bothered to rinse them before opening them and there was a lil' sand & grit on them. Mme Moulin informed me that it was traditional to eat raw oysters and drink white wine at New Year's dinners. After opening the shell, the oyster is left inside & a little bit of lemon juice is squeezed onto the oyster to make it retract so it'll be easier to pluck from its shell and slide it into one's mouth. I had already resolved that I wasn't going to eat any of that because - No.1 - I don't care for raw meat; No. 2 - eating a live animal is cruel, and No.3 - I had tasted a fried oyster about 4 yrs earlier and even with being fried it tasted like a cold ball of ~~snort~~ snot. Well we soon sat down to eat; it was about 8:30pm. The French have long New Year's dinners. They like to pass into the New Year while dining w/ their families. The table was set w/oysters, wine, crab, pickles, ham, pork, rabbit & pigeon meat & fish, & rillette de canard, bread & homemade mayonnaise. I tasted the crab but didn't like it. Mme Moulin's mayonnaise was really good, and I had my fair share of it w/bread. I refused the wine so they gave me some fruit juice. Let me mention here that a tradition at New Year's dinners is to taste diff. kinds of wines & champagne. They tasted about 5 diff. kinds of wine including a bottle of California wine before dinner was over. I had some pickles & ham and pork & ~~duck meat~~

3

I also tasted the pigeon and rabbit meat; it was alright. It amazed me how they really went at eating those oysters. Mme Moulin ate about 20 or 25 & her husband had about 30 to 35. His brothers had their share too, and a friend of Mr. Moulin was just eating them & chunking the shells in a pan on the floor like he was shelling beans & throwing the hulls in a bag. My! My! My!!! The poor sea creatures! And then again, what did one of the children behold in one of the shells from which the oyster had been eaten — another little red worm, alive & crawling! Well, this course of the meal lasted about an hour. Then two big bowls were brought out — one with salad & the other with corn & green & red bell pepper. The corn dish was pretty good. We also ate some tangerines & oranges. Then it was decided that we would watch a comical film that had been videotaped. It was about a mailman in a small French village during the 50's who was trying to imitate the speed of the American postal system with his bicycle. It was chic to do things the American way after the Second World War since America was the dominant power & was looked up to. The film was really funny. We started watching it at about 10:30pm since we didn't want to finish the meal before the New Year arrived. Film ended at about 11:30pm. Everyone back to the table for the next course — cheese & bread. Well, while we were watching the film, my stomach had become slightly upset with me about what I had eaten & began to let me know it even more as I sat back down to the table.

Came back to table & Mme Moulin gave me

some baking soda in warm water to settle my stomach. It calmed its wave of anger, but I didn't dare add anything else to make it mad again. They started serving dessert & the first thing brought out was a birthday cake for M. Moulin. He was born at 1:15am on Jan. 1 & was 44 yrs old. The cake had been made by his mother & had 3 layers (2 even layers & topped off with a center third layer a bit larger). It was topped with peanuts & toffee frosting — inner layers also had toffee frosting between them. It looked really good. Mme Moulin added 4 small sth olive green candles to the top layer — each standing for 10 yrs & 4 shorter but fatter candles to the two bottom layers — each symbolizing 1 yr. M. Moulin blew them out w/two strong breaths & his second oldest brother cut the cake & served everyone. Then, it was time for Christmas Pudding — an English specialty. Mme Moulin had made one & bought one from Lyon to compare others. It was served warm w/cream & looked good. Thus, we had had a French-English-American dinner. Oh, Mme. Moulin had also made some English mince pies which are served at English Christmas dinners & of which two are left by the chimney for the Père Noel in England the night before Christmas. We had passed into the '89 year while dining & it was now about 1:30am. We talked a bit more as M. Moulin opened his birthday presents. Actually, we had celebrated 3 occasions — the anniversary of the second brother & his wife (Dec. 31); New Year's; and M. Moulin's birthday. It had been joyous!! Mme Moulin & her sister-in-law drove me home; it was about 2am. I came into my room & got ready for bed. I awoke this morning at about 8am but didn't get up till after 10am. Mme Moulin had prepared a container of desserts for me since I couldn't eat any last night. I had tangerines, mince pies, & 2 slices of birthday cake.

5

I really liked the mince pies; I had 3 of them. The cake was good too though I'm not too fond of tofee. I'm now getting ready to heat up the Christmas pudding & have it w/cream. Then, I'll go to the afternoon's church service & thank God for crossing over into another year!

Jan. 1 - evening

Well, I went to church at 3:30, but there was no service but a small reception for New Year's. Few people were there. We drank tea, coffee, fruit juice, & Coca-Cola and ate some cakes that the assistant minister's wife had prepared. It was good. Afterwards, we sang songs. The minister's wife sang one in English — "Why Should I Feel Discouraged?" Also sang "What A Friend," "How Great Thou Art," and some other songs in French. Then played some games w/kids, cleared up & cleaned up & I returned home at about 6:30 pm. I enjoyed the fellowship.

While there, this scripture came to me:

"Behold, I lay a stone in Zion." (Isaiah 28.16).

Feb. 26, 1989   excursion

Went on a "ballade" w/Hazel, the Asst. d'anglais at Jules Ferry college who lives at hotel here & one of the English teachers at her college & her husband. Also, two other men, one of whom was very cultured. Departed from Vichy, Source des Célestins, between 1:15 & 1:30 pm & headed for the ruins of an old château (château de Tournoël) in Volvic which is between Riom & Clermont-Ferrand. I rode w/the English teacher & her husband & we had some interesting discussions about the history of France (religion, kings, etc.) & also about the U.S. (education at university level). We passed thru several small towns, one of which was Randan, & stopped in Riom to pick up an elderly couple who were friends of the man who was leading the voyage. They were very nice. We arrived in Volvic & stopped at one of the tourist centers which was closed. We walked around & looked at the stones which consisted of volcanic lava. Two kinds — one was red & spongy & soft

& is called "pouzolane". The other is darkish gray & is harder; as it becomes old, it blackens. Many of the buildings in the region have this lava in their construction & around the windows. After visiting the château & walking around it, we went to a ~~small~~ village called Châtel-Guyon to have warm drinks & pâtisseries. The weather was cold & windy & it was snowing. I didn't eat or drink anything but looked at a map of Auvergne to locate the château & river mentioned in <u>L'Astrée</u>. I was told that I could take the train to Thiers & then go to Boën (château supposedly 6km from Boën). We ~~then~~ went to Riom & walked around in the city to look at some old houses dating back to the Renaissance & also an old church there. We then dropped off the couple we had picked up there & headed back to Vichy. Arrived back at ~7pm. It was a superb day; I learned a lot & was overwhelmed w/the beauty of the skyline & clouds! What a Creator!
P.S. - I picked up some lava rock in Volvic for souvenirs.

April 7, 1989
Went on a short voyage to Thiers, a city about 35 km to the southeast of Vichy. Mr ~~Thiers~~ Thierry, a teacher at a lycée in Thiers, had offered to drive me & the other assistante d'anglais at hôtel here there. Assistant's name Hazel Cock. Mr Georges ~~Thiers~~ Thierry is the husband of the German teacher at my college & their son, Alexandre Thierry, is in my class of 4e2 (Langue 2).

We left from Vichy at approx. 9:30am. I prayed that I would have no problems w/my stomach or head. Today is Friday & I had had problems w/my stomach on Tuesday & Wednesday, because I had not eaten properly being that we were on Easter vacation from school. However, Wednesday

April 7 (cont'd)

evening I had gone to the usual Bible study & prayer meeting at 6pm w/ the Nigerian brothers (& sister) from the church (two brothers from the West Indies were also there) & one brother from Uganda. After studying James 3, we had prayed & the Lord had touched my stomach & absolved the pain. On Thursday, I awoke w/a headache but refused to be subdued. At 12pm Hazel & I went to an English professor's house to eat lunch. Her name is Mme. Granvau & she teaches at the "école supérieure-courrere féminine" near byu hotel. We had read some tourist articles in English for her at the school's laboratory-rue sornin. Thus, they were recorded for the students' exams of English comprehension. Thus, inviting us to lunch was her way of thanking us. We had some peanut butter curlies while waiting for lunch. Lunch was shrimp w/eyes, tail, etc., radishes, bread, mushroom paste, butter, and rice w/fish w/a peppermint leaf inside. The fish was cooked whole - head & tail. Even the eyes were still there, looking like small white marbles because they had popped out from their sockets. I don't like eating things which still possess their head & tail! Then we had cheese & bread & last a strawberry pie. All in all it was good though I wouldn't eat much because I had a headache & didn't want to upset my stomach again. Afterwards, we talked for about 5 hrs. & she drove us home at 6pm.

Now, let me get back on track w/today. When I awoke

this morning, I felt good. My headache was gone. As we were going towards Thiers, Mr Therre pointed out many interesting houses & made comments about their origin of style & other historical facts. Stopped in a small village to give a paper to one of his students. We arrived in Thiers at about 10:15 am. Thiers is very hilly w/ narrow streets & is smaller but older than Vichy. We toured the streets w/ Mr Therre acting as our guide. He was excellent & an expert. We looked at several houses dating back to the 15th & 16th centuries. Also saw a house where Blaise Pascal stayed for some days when he was ~12 yrs. old. Saw lots of doors w/ symbols such as leaves or statues of the 16th & 17th century. Lots of things that I had studied really came to life. Then we went in the "Maison des Couteliers" & was shown how & what effort went into making the knives. Then toured the museum upstairs, led by Mr Therre whose guide was very informative. We finished about noon. Bought postcards & went to eat in a nearby restaurant - Restaurant Aux Folies Bérbères. I had spaghetti w/ mushrooms & mushroom cream & French fries. Hazel had couscous w/ chicken & Mr Therre had fries w/ a brochette grillée. They had coffee afterwards. I had water the whole time. I believe I ate too much. However, my stomach was reasonable w/ me. We then looked at a few other things in the streets & went to meet a lady who is a German teacher in Clermont-Ferrand. We went to another building of the Couteliers for her to buy gifts. The people there were super nice. They sat down, talked, made coffee for us, & gave us gifts for coming. We parted, went to a shop where they made only "virolés" (part of knife between blade & handle). Lady gave us calendars. We drove German teacher back to her car & we looked at an old church - St Genès. That was end of town. It was ~5:10pm. Oh! also watched man polishing knife w/ dog on his back in another part of the Couteliers. (cont'd)

April 7 (cont'd)

On way back Mr Therre showed us a house which had been hit by rocks being fired at Germans during WWII. Also stopped in Châteldon to see a château. Later on the road saw a cross (very old) engraved w/ lilies & another château which had been bought by & was inhabited by a Canadian. Arrived in Vichy at ~6 p.m. Had a wonderful, inspiring, fulfilling, cultural day. I truly enjoyed it! I must now write Mr Therre a thank-you note.

May 15, 1989 – Voyage à Bën s/Lignon

Left at ~1:05 pm from Vichy w/ Mr. Therre et son fils Alexandre Therre qui est dans ma classe de 4°2 pour visiter la Bastie d'Urfé. It was nice to get away from Vichy for a few hours. On the way stopped at a hospital on outskirts of Thiers which was fairly new. We looked at an exposition on the history of the hospital. Included in the exposition was a valise of Mme Elisabeth, sister of Louis XVI. She had spent a few days at this hospital during the Revolution & someone had found this suitcase w/her name engraved on it. (very recently) Continued en route. Stopped in Noirétable for Mr Therre to look for a newspaper - all shops were closed. A little before, he stopped to take a picture of a soldier painted red, white, & blue. The paysage was extraordinaire et le temps était impeccable. There were lots of rocky mtns. w/ fiery yellow flowers. Arrived in Bën at ~3 pm. Visited château & walked in gardens & took pictures. Certain articles of the château had been sold by former propriétaire & were in a museum in New York. Left château at approx. 4:30 pm & went to a part of the Lignon near château & took more pictures. Ate some petits gâteaux at picnic table beside Lignon avant (I took a rock from the Lignon as a souvenir.)   (cont'd)

May 15 (cont'd)

de partir. It did me good all in my toes to see the things I had studied in Dr. Daniel's 17th century novel class in Fall 1986. At ~5:30 headed back. Stopped in Noretable & looked at a church where two names of Theure family who died in WWI were inscribed on wall of church & on a monument near church. Stopped also in Cervieres, a former fortified town & visited an artisan shop w/lots of homemade products. Returned to Vichy at ~7:15pm. Superb day!!

www.ingramcontent.com/pod-product-compliance
Lightning Source LLC
Chambersburg PA
CBHW041152290426
44108CB00002B/48